Changed from GLORY *into* GLORY

Changed from Glory *into* Glory

Wesleyan Prayer for Transformation

PAUL WESLEY CHILCOTE

NASHVILLE

Changed from Glory into Glory
Wesleyan Prayer for Transformation

The Upper Room® Web site: www.upperroom.org.

Cover and interior design: GoreStudio Inc.
Cover image: *The Angelus* by Jean-François Millet. Musée d'Orsay, Paris/SuperStock
First printing: 2005

Library of Congress Cataloging-in-Publication Data
Chilcote, Paul Wesley, 1954–
Changed from glory into glory : Wesleyan prayer for transformation / Paul Wesley Chilcote.
p. cm.
ISBN 0-8358-9814-8
1. Prayer—Christianity. 2. Methodist Church—Prayer books and devotions—English. I. Title.
BV210.3.C46 2005
248.3'2—dc22 2005011651

Printed in the United States of America.

In memoriam
MARK GIBBARD, SSJE

and for
the Monastic Community of Mount Angel Abbey,
especially
ODO RECKER, OSB
and
BERNARD SANDER, OSB
fellow pilgrims in the life of prayer

Lex orandi, Lex credendi

Contents

Introduction

A Journey toward RESTORATION

Glory! The gospel of our Lord Jesus Christ reflects the glory of God. It has to do with the freedom and glory that are ours in the new life offered to us in Christ. Paul focused his attention on this theme in the third chapter of his second letter to the Corinthians. God's self-revelation came through Moses in such a way that the people of Israel could not even gaze at him because of the glory of his face. "How much more," says Paul, "will the ministry of the Spirit come in glory?" He contrasts the Old Covenant with the New in Christ as if to say, "If you thought that was glorious, you haven't seen anything yet!" Life in Christ is glorious! Being a Christian entails living in and becoming transparent to God's glory.

Paul concludes this chapter with one of the most remarkable statements in the New Testament:

> And all of us, with unveiled faces, seeing the glory of the Lord as though reflected in a mirror, are being transformed into the same image from one degree of glory to another; for this comes from the Lord, the Spirit.

Charles Wesley conveyed this vision of a glorious Christian life in his great hymn "Love Divine, All Loves Excelling":

Changed from glory into glory,
Till in heaven we take our place,
Till we cast our crowns before thee,
Lost in wonder, love, and praise.[1]

The title of this book comes from that first line. Wesley was giving expression to the same vision of transformation, change, renewal, and restoration that Paul experienced. I hope this is your vision of what it means to be a Christian; if your view of the faith is something different, perhaps this study will be an encouragement to you as you consider these amazing possibilities.

Nothing in this vision is burdensome. It might be hard going at times, but that is the case with any relationship worth keeping. Nothing in this vision concerns what you or I can attain through our own efforts, because Christian life is about what God has done through Christ and what God can do in the Spirit. Most importantly, and while not explicitly mentioned by either Paul or Wesley, a life changed from glory into glory—a life lost in wonder, love, and praise—is a life necessarily rooted in prayer. This book is about becoming so rooted.

Great People of Prayer

How many great people of prayer have you known? I have encountered many followers of Christ for whom prayer formed the very core of their being. But several stand out. I met Brother Mark Gibbard in Africa. My family and I were involved in mission service in Kenya when this Anglican monk came to our seminary to conduct a monastic retreat for our community. I will never forget that holy time. For a whole week we prayed together, studied God's Word together, and grew so much closer to one another. I remember the steady stream of students who went to see Brother Mark for spiritual counsel. The depth of insight in this true Christian elder came from a life spent praying the Word.

Howard Thurman is another witness who comes into my mind. I first met this radiant African-American Quaker when I was a seminary student at Duke Divinity School. He made a number of formal presentations to the entire seminary community, but I remember most vividly the informal conversations he and I shared on the periphery of the main events. I was absolutely fixated on his every word. Whenever he talked about God his eyes sparkled and danced as though he had been filled with positive, life-giving energy. His joy and total engagement with life were contagious. "In life there is nothing more important than prayer," he admonished me on one occasion. "God has created us in such a way that everything we do flows from our center—our heart. Make sure that your heart belongs to God."

Some great men and women of prayer who have affected me the most are part of a great cloud of witnesses I will never meet in this life. One in particular is an early Methodist woman in England by the name of Ann Cutler. All who knew her called her "Praying Nanny," for none was so noted for her prayer as this great woman of faith. Stories about her life of prayer were spread far and wide even during her lifetime. Her pattern of prayer was unusual for any person of any time. She prayed as often as twelve to fourteen times a day. Her biographer, William Bramwell, described her public prayers as simple and artless, but they were powerful and awakening at the same time. In fact, her prayers seemed to pour new life into floundering Methodist Societies and into people who had lost their passion for Christ. Bramwell testified to the fact that he never expected to see her equal in prayer again.

Foundations of the Journey

I hope this little book will help you wherever you happen to be in your life of prayer, in your journey of transformation from one degree of glory into another. If you feel like a novice in this great pilgrimage into a closer walk with God (the way most of us happen to feel if we are honest with ourselves), you may find some helpful guidance as you seek to take first steps. On the other hand, if you are experienced in the ways of prayer, I think you will find wonderful resources here to deepen your relationship with God in Christ. Regardless of how far you have come or how far you need to go, you have an amazing companion in the person of the Holy Spirit, who is most certainly our only real teacher in the life of prayer.

Two important aspects of the Christian story undergird this study of prayer. First, the event of the Transfiguration functions as an important paradigm of the Christian life for me. This mountaintop experience and Jesus' immediate descent into life's valley (discussed fully in chapter 1) establish a pattern of prayer to keep in the back of your mind throughout this sacred journey. Each successive chapter builds upon this foundation and opens new understandings about the connection between prayer and life.

Second, the entire study reflects the centrality of the death and resurrection of Jesus (the original proclamation, or *kerygma*, of the church) in prayer. Our life of prayer is shaped more than anything else by the core belief that Jesus Christ "suffered under Pontius Pilate, was crucified, dead, and buried" and that "the third day he rose from the dead." Prayer always moves from death to life because it truly reflects life in Christ, and this pattern shapes both the whole and the parts of this study as well. We will walk together, therefore, through some of the most momentous events that shape our lives as Christians.

How to Use This Book

You can make your journey through this book in different ways. You may read and meditate upon the material over the course of eight weeks, reading a chapter each week. Each chapter consists of

- scripture texts designed to shape your thoughts and prayers for the week
- a narrative discussion of the scripture
- a hymn text by Charles Wesley
- reflection on a work of art
- a meditation

You are free to use these materials in whatever ways help you to come close to God in prayer. You may want to read the biblical passage daily or use the hymn, art, and meditation in the same way. Contemplating art offers a powerful way to enter into a relationship with God in prayer. Many people find that keeping a spiritual journal enhances that relationship. You could record your reactions and responses to the readings or artwork in a journal and reflect upon them at the end of the week, noting how God has challenged you, stretched you, sustained you, nourished you.

Various eight-week blocks of time in the course of the year could be especially appropriate for this reflective study. Launch the year with a renewed commitment to your life of prayer, using January–February as a period of renewal. Or refresh yourself during two months in the summer. Use the season of Pentecost as an opportunity to invite the Holy Spirit into your prayer life once again.

This book can also be used over the course of an eight-day week, Sunday through Sunday. There is much merit in this approach. Holy Week, the period between Palm/Passion Sunday and Easter, would be a natural week to immerse yourself in this material, especially given the underlying theme of our movement from death to resurrection. You could actually live out this paradigm of the life in Christ—from glory to glory—concluding on the "Eighth Day" with a glorious experience of resurrected life in the Lord. This approach, in fact, could be used during any week of the entire year, since movement from creation and through death to resurrection is the normal rhythm of our Christian life as a whole. Every Sunday is a "little Easter," and any week fits naturally into the pattern.

If used over an eight-day period, I would recommend that each chapter function as a morning prayer experience, perhaps repeating the hymn and/or meditation at the end of the day. Using this material over the course of one week will also give you a panoramic vision of prayer. Identify a specific week during the year and consecrate it to the sacred task of growing closer to God through this study. You may also find it helpful to dip back into this book from time to time, to refresh your life of prayer and your communion with the Lord. While designed primarily for individual use, you could utilize this book in small groups, Sunday school classes, or even as a churchwide study as well.

Use as a Lenten Study

The eight-week period of the Lenten season offers a perfect time frame for this immersion in prayer. If used during Lent, I suggest you begin the study on Transfiguration Sunday, the Sunday prior to Ash Wednesday. By devoting each week in Lent to a chapter, you will conclude the study with the celebration of the Resurrection on Easter Sunday. Obviously any time is a good time to pray, but if you are seeking a deeper walk with Christ, no time could be better than this season. The followers of Christ have "kept this time" precisely for this reason for nearly two millennia now. So you are in good company.

However you decide to use this book, take plenty of time for prayer and meditation. Establishing that priority in your life is the most important step. Pray as you begin. Pray as you close. Exercise and rest as much as possible. Remember that God is pure, universal love. God is merciful and slow to anger. God is the powerful, awesome Creator of all that is. God is glorious. God loves you.

1

The Rhythm of the TRANSFIGURATION

Now about eight days after these sayings Jesus took with him Peter and John and James, and went up on the mountain to pray. And while he was praying, the appearance of his face changed, and his clothes became dazzling white. Suddenly they saw two men, Moses and Elijah, talking to him. They appeared in glory and were speaking of his departure, which he was about to accomplish at Jerusalem. Now Peter and his companions were weighed down with sleep; but since they had stayed awake, they saw his glory and the two men who stood with him. Just as they were leaving him, Peter said to Jesus, "Master, it is good for us to be here; let us make three dwellings, one for you, one for Moses, and one for Elijah"—not knowing what he said. While he was saying this, a cloud came and overshadowed them; and they were terrified as they entered the cloud. Then from the cloud came a voice that said, "This is my Son, my Chosen; listen to him!" When the voice had spoken, Jesus was found alone. And they kept silent and in those days told no one any of the things they had seen.

On the next day, when they had come down from the mountain, a great crowd met him. Just

> then a man from the crowd shouted, "Teacher, I beg you to look at my son; he is my only child. Suddenly a spirit seizes him, and all at once he shrieks. It convulses him until he foams at the mouth; it mauls him and will scarcely leave him...." Jesus answered, "... Bring your son here." While he was coming, the demon dashed him to the ground in convulsions. But Jesus rebuked the unclean spirit, healed the boy, and gave him back to his father. And all were astounded at the greatness of God.—*Luke 9:28-39, 41-43*

Jesus was a man of prayer. He linked prayer directly with life and helped people in two particular ways in his effort to guide those he loved into a restored and intimate relationship with God. First, he taught people about himself, in the Sermon on the Mount, for example. Whenever people encountered Jesus, they discovered the true nature of God. Jesus reflected the divine through both his words and his actions. In statements such as the "I am" sayings of the Gospel of John he described himself as "the way, and the truth, and the life," "the good shepherd," the "true vine," and "the resurrection and the life," among other things. Through his teachings about himself Jesus demonstrated the fact that all of life is prayer and love.

Second, Jesus helped people to know him as a special and close friend. Those closest to him during his lifetime came to know about prayer through the way Jesus related to them, through the shaping influence of friendship. In one instance, he took three disciples from the noisy villages to the silent top of the Mount of Transfiguration to pray. And what an amazing experience of prayer they all had there. Just think for a few moments about the richness of the event itself.

The Event of the Transfiguration

The Transfiguration was of central importance in the life of our Lord. Perhaps even more significantly, it shaped the lives of Jesus' three most intimate companions. The event as a whole richly illustrates great themes of our faith. It represents a critical juncture in the life of Christ that looks both backward and forward. It focuses our attention on the past, on earlier events in the life of Jesus and, indeed, on the central acts of God among the Hebrew people. At the same time, it points to the future, to the fulfillment of God's redemptive purpose in Jesus Christ.

Perhaps you have had a mountaintop experience with God or long for a dramatic, monumental moment that will shape the rest of your life. Certainly the Transfiguration is Jesus' mountaintop experience if he ever had one! And we cannot help being reminded of that great mountain scene of the Old Testament—of Moses on Mount Sinai—of Moses' encounter with God in the burning bush. At the same time, however, the Transfiguration anticipates the triumphant glorification of Christ. It points to his victorious resurrection and ascension from the Mount of Olives. Mountains always signify those places where we meet God. In prayer we ascend into the presence of God. We lift up our hearts to the Lord. Every time of prayer—every moment spent in prayer—is an opportunity to encounter God in the fullness of God's glory.

Think for a moment about the central figures in this scene. Moses was the prototype of the Messiah—the great deliverer, the embodiment of the Law. Elijah was the forerunner of the Messiah, the greatest of the prophets, whose name itself means "the Lord he is God." The Transfiguration reveals and confirms that Jesus is the Messiah, the fulfillment of both the Law and the Prophets. In Luke's Gospel, this mountaintop event immediately follows the account of Peter's bold proclamation that Jesus is "the Messiah of God" (Luke 9:20).

Yet another perspective. The Transfiguration reflects back the baptism of Jesus, that point in Jesus' life when he began to realize his vocation as the Messiah. Indeed, God's confirmation of the Son at his baptism is echoed here unmistakably in the words "This is my Son, my Chosen [Beloved]" (Luke 9:35). But at the same time, the Transfiguration announces the fulfillment of Christ's mission as the Suffering Servant of God. It points to the culmination of his self-sacrificing love in his passion and death. At Jesus' baptism he began to envision his life's mission; the Transfiguration confirmed the only way by which that mission of love was to be fulfilled.

A Pattern of Prayer

But what does all of this have to do with prayer? The Transfiguration—the event as a whole—provides a pattern for us, a paradigm of prayer worth emulating in our own lives. The pattern essentially presents contemplation and action. It points us to an understanding of prayer that incorporates both catching a glimpse of the divine and translating that vision into action in the life of the world. We see this rhythm throughout Jesus' life. This is the kind of prayer he lived. I call this the rhythm of the Transfiguration, and I want you to focus your attention on this pattern in the first step of our journey together into prayer.

A Glimpse of the Divine

The single most significant fact regarding the disciples in this story is that they caught a glimpse of the divine. They encountered the living God in Christ. What Peter had confessed with his lips he now experienced as a reality in his life. And you can be assured that any glimpse of the divine, no matter how fleeting or momentary, is life-transforming. The essence of prayer involves personal encounter with God and God's transformation of our lives. In the Transfiguration the true meaning of Jesus the Christ—the eternal reality embodied in him—was glimpsed, for a moment at least, by the disciples.

> Who tastes the truth, and Jesus sees
> In all the Scripture-mysteries
> The law and prophets' End,
> Delights to meditate and pray,
> Would gladly on the mountain stay,
> And never more descend.[1]

Little wonder that Peter blurted out, "Master, it is good for us to be here." In *The Message,* Eugene Peterson says tersely: "Master, this is a great moment!" Little wonder that impetuous Peter wanted to prolong the experience by providing three dwellings for Jesus and his heavenly companions. Jesus' life no longer appeared "normal" but was momentarily invested with the brilliance and power of God. Peter saw Jesus in his glory. He experienced a glimpse of the divine, and that experience of God in Christ literally transformed his life.

Have you ever had a glimpse of the divine? This is what the life of prayer is all about. Have you ever looked at a simple, ordinary object a thousand times, and now for the very first time really see it? Prayer enables us to find God in every aspect of life. Have you ever looked into the face of a friend, your spouse, your child, and now for the very first time really see him or her? Harry Haines, former director of the United Methodist Committee on Relief, preached at my church immediately following a momentous trip to Calcutta. He recounted his introduction to Mother Teresa. He entered her "sanctuary" where she cared for the dying and saw her holding a little baby in her arms. As Harry stepped forward to greet her, Mother Teresa carefully thrust the infant into his arms and said, "Look into his precious face. Can you not see Christ in this little child of God?" That was an act of prayer. The most pertinent fact about the disciples in this story is that they experienced a glimpse of the divine! These kinds of experiences are central to prayer. I will be talking more about this throughout the study. Whenever you catch a glimpse of the divine, you cannot be the same. God's transforming power is at work in your life.

Translating Vision into Action

The second half of the pattern of prayer, however, is as important as the first. The life of prayer must be characterized by the translation of this vision of God—our glimpse of the divine—into action. Peter, not knowing what he said, wanted to remain on the mountaintop. Wouldn't it be nice for our life to be one great, continuous mountaintop experience? There is such a strong, and not so subtle, temptation to want to bask in God's glory and love. But prayer is a larger reality than this. Rather than leaving us passive, true prayer moves us to act. As one of the earliest Christian hymns proclaims of our Pattern:

> Though [Christ Jesus] was in the form of God,
> [he] did not regard equality with God
> as something to be exploited,
> but emptied himself,
> taking the form of a slave,
> being born in human likeness.
> And being found in human form,
> he humbled himself

> and became obedient to the point of death—
> even death on a cross. (Phil. 2:6-8)

Our glimpse of the divine, our vision of God, our understanding of the reign of God in human history must be translated into action.

Nowhere is this imperative more striking than in Luke's Gospel where the the story of Christ healing a boy with epilepsy immediately follows the Transfiguration. Reading these two accounts together, we notice the contrast between them could not be more dramatic. In place of the mountain's solitude, a great crowd sets the context for action. Instead of Moses and Elijah with Jesus in glory, a worried father with his afflicted son confront Jesus. A complaint about the weakness and failure of Jesus' disciples displaces a reassuring voice from heaven. Jesus has just been communing with God in glory; now he must deal with a demon.

The message comes through clearly: the One whom God approved on the mountaintop is he through whom God now acts in the dark valleys of life. The way of Jesus is not a detached glory but a glory relevant and active in the most sordid of human situations. Jesus shines all the more clearly as his actions illuminate the dark spaces in which people live. He gets his hands dirty in the world of everyday life and transforms it by his presence. The way of Jesus is to be pierced by the hatred and cruelty of those he came to save and to go on loving. You and I are called to nothing less!

Raphael Captures the Pattern

The great Renaissance artist Raphael captured the rhythm of the Transfiguration—this movement from contemplation to action—in the last product of his creative genius.

(See Plate 1 in Illustrations.) The painting is divided into two parts. While the upper portion of this great work of art depicts the Transfiguration of Christ, the lower part portrays the agony of the father and his son with epilepsy, surrounded by the crowd, including some of Jesus' other followers. In this scene the father, robed in green to symbolize hope, presents his son to the disciples. The father supports the boy, who cannot stand because a seizure grips him.

According to art historians, the painting speaks volumes in its symbolism. Raphael depicts the Transfiguration and the healing in tandem, thus joining the transfigured Christ and the boy afflicted with epilepsy. This broken human being, who falls to the ground in a seizure and lies there as if dead, is risen to newness of life through Christ—a dramatic foreshadowing of the movement from crucifixion to resurrection in the life of Christ himself. Only the boy in the lower portion of the picture turns his face to the transfigured Christ in the upper part of the painting. So it is the boy in need of healing who establishes the link between the painting's two parts.[2]

Few commentators have observed the potent paradigm in the connection of these two accounts—the Transfiguration and the healing. In the conjunction of these two stories we are offered a pattern for life, a pattern for prayer. This pattern safeguards us from the dangers of holding on to half the truth without embracing its complementary counterpart. Prayer is not meant to be only a series of mountaintop experiences. While nothing supersedes our communion with God—our experience of God's glory and love—prayer separated from active, self-giving service to others can become a dangerous idolatry. Remember the Pharisees! On the other hand, if our active service aims at anything other than the glory of God, it can become a source of self-righteousness that actually distances us from the God we seek to serve in others. But when held together—when our contemplation of God's glory leads us to acts of loving service—abundant life breaks in upon us. We discover once again what life is all about.

"'Twixt the Mount and Multitude"

Charles Wesley had learned this pattern of prayer early in life. He sang about it in many of his hymns. One of his hymns in particular, directly related to the Transfiguration of Christ, describes this life in lyric simplicity and profundity. One stanza explains:

> While thou didst on earth appear,
> Servant to thy servants here,
> Mindful of thy place above,
> All thy life was prayer and love.[3]

Wesley talks about the importance of holding faith and love together, how we fully realize our secret communion with God in prayer through works of love and mercy for others. He describes another rhythm of our "praying Pattern," namely, the need to meet with God regularly in morning and evening devotions, a pattern of prayer we'll consider later. Reflecting on the Transfiguration and healing account, he describes our life in Christ—our life of prayer—as something we live out "'twixt the mount and multitude." What a marvelous image! We live out our lives as vessels, as instruments of grace, in the continual movement between the mountain and the multitude—between moments in which we glimpse the glory of God and times in which we love and give and serve for God's glory. This is the rhythm of the Transfiguration.

As you move through this series of meditations, my prayer is that you will find new ways to live out this pattern of prayer. To practice the presence of God requires precisely that: practice and intentionality. Spend quality time with God. Seek God's presence. Your experience of God's glory may be dramatic at times. On other occasions, you may encounter the glory of God in that still, small voice in the innermost part of your being. But as you seek to commune intimately with God, make sure that you find ways of translating those experiences, that relationship, into action. Think about the ways in which God is calling you to serve others. They may, in fact undoubtedly will, call for sacrifice. To permit God to mobilize you for action may stretch you beyond your comfort zone. But find some avenue of active service in which to engage as you progress through the chapters in this book. Jesus served the poor. Perhaps ministries in your church or community provide such opportunities for you. Take courage. When you embrace the possibilities, you will be amazed at how God will transform your entire life into an act of prayer.

Hymn

Holy Lamb, Who Thee Confess

Holy Lamb, who thee confess,
Followers of thy holiness,
Thee they ever keep in view,
Ever ask, "What shall we do?"

Governed by thy only will,
All thy words we would fulfil,
Would in all thy footsteps go,
Walk as Jesus walked below.

While thou didst on earth appear,
Servant to thy servants here,
Mindful of thy place above,
All thy life was prayer and love.

Such our whole employment be:
Works of faith and charity,
Works of love on man bestowed,
Secret intercourse with God.

Early in the temple met,
Let us still our Saviour greet;
Nightly to the mount repair,
Join our praying Pattern there.

There by wrestling faith obtain
Power to work for God again,
Power his image to retrieve,
Power like thee, our Lord, to live.

Vessels, instruments of grace,
Pass we thus our happy days
'Twixt the mount and multitude,
Doing or receiving good:

Glad to pray and labour on
Till our earthly course is run,
Till we on the sacred tree
Bow the head, and die like thee.[4]

Meditation

The Transfiguration

Lord, you are with me now.
I see you, Lord, with the disciples,
leaving the noise of the villages.
I see the disciples climbing up into the quietness
of the high mountain.
Lord, help me now to leave behind
the noise and pressures of my ordinary life.
Lord, help me to think deeply about you.
Help me to stay with you like a close friend.
Help me to be glad to spend all these
quiet moments close to you.
Lord, you said, "Abide in me,
and I in you; abide in my love."
This is what I truly want to do.
This will help me to become a better Christian.
Amen.

2

The Nature of PRAYER

So deeply do we care for you that we are determined to share with you not only the gospel of God but also our own selves, because you have become very dear to us.—*1 Thessalonians 2:8*

Beloved, let us love one another, because love is from God; everyone who loves is born of God and knows God. Whoever does not love does not know God, for God is love. God's love was revealed among us in this way: God sent his only Son into the world so that we might live through him. In this is love, not that we loved God but that he loved us and sent his Son to be the atoning sacrifice for our sins. Beloved, since God loved us so much, we also ought to love one another. No one has ever seen God; if we love one another, God lives in us, and his love is perfected in us.

By this we know that we abide in him and he in us, because he has given us of his Spirit. And we have seen and do testify that the Father has sent his Son as the Savior of the world. God abides in those who confess that Jesus is the Son of God, and they abide in God. So we have known and believe the love that God has for us.

God is love, and those who abide in love abide in God, and God abides in them.—*1 John 4:7-16*

All Christians need to pray. We are by nature pray-ers. Prayer is like the air we breathe. Without prayer we quickly become less than what God created us to be. But it is also beneficial for us to grow in prayer. Jesus' disciples acknowledged their need for growth and instruction in this area of their lives. On one occasion when Jesus had spent time in prayer and returned to his followers, the disciples said to him, "Lord, teach us to pray, as John taught his disciples" (Luke 11:1). Jesus responded with what we now call the Lord's Prayer. This model prayer gave those who yearned to cultivate a deeper spirituality a pattern into which they could grow. It is not enough to pray. We need to grow in prayer; otherwise, our human potentialities will remain undiscovered and undeveloped. Prayer creates intimacy with God and reveals to us who we really are.

Prayer as Abiding

Prayer is not primarily asking but abiding. It has to do with staying close to the Lord. There may be no more intimate image in the Bible in terms of our relationship with God through Christ than the image of abiding. John particularly lifts up this image, repeatedly linking the image to love.

As we have just read in 1 John: "God is love, and those who abide in love abide in God, and God abides in them." John 15 probably develops the idea of abiding in Christ most fully. Here Jesus gives us the image of the vine and the branches. The whole phrase—"abide in me as I abide in you"—has an imperative tone in this context. Whatever leads to this intimacy with the Lord is good; whatever creates barriers to this abiding is bad. Abiding is the ultimate object of all forms of Christian worship and discipleship. An intimate fellowship with

Jesus constitutes the life of the Christian: to abide in Christ and he in us. That means we must permit God's love in Christ to enfold us in its embrace. To abide in Christ wraps us in this love. And as we abide in Christ, this love becomes a pervasive atmosphere. It becomes the very breath of our lives. This dynamic relationship—abiding in the love of the God we have come to know in Jesus—defines our life of prayer.

This concept of abiding is actually deeply rooted in our Christian view of God. While One in essence, God is also in community with God's self. We call this reality the Trinity: God, One in Three and Three in One. Andrei Rublev's *Icon of the Holy Trinity* is one of the most well-known works of art in the Russian Orthodox tradition. (See Plate 2 in Illustrations.) The story of the visit of three angels to Abraham and his wife, Sarah, in Genesis 18 inspired the painting's creator. In this significant story in the narrative of the Hebrew people the angels herald news of a son (Isaac) who will be born to the aged couple. Traditional Orthodox theologians view this Old Testament event as a foreshadowing of God's full revelation of self in the New Testament. The angels of the icon represent the three persons of the Trinity: God the Father, God the Son, and God the Holy Spirit. The artist depicts the iconic figures as equals around the table of this interaction. Their unity in diversity makes this work of art unique.

Commentators describe the Trinitarian persons as gentle, quiet, anxious, and sorrowful. A meditative, contemplative, detached-yet-intimate mood characterizes the icon. Rublev strikes a masterful balance between the material and the spiritual. Anyone who meditates upon the icon enters a timeless world without beginning and without end. The icon projects infinite and eternal qualities. The attitudes, gestures, and positions of the Three suggest a symmetry or harmony of life in community. The icon leaves the clear impression of harmonious interaction, synchronized dance, mutual interdependence—abiding.[1]

In this eternal paradigm of abiding, each member of the Trinity expresses love through trust in the others. God is portrayed as a true community of love. The icon radiates love. And this love is communicated to those who meditate upon the image with its compelling, even magnetic force. We are drawn into the joy and wonder and mystery of the God of love. Rublev's icon powerfully manifests the nature of prayer. Prayer is abiding.

Prayer as Friendship

Prayer also concerns friendship. I can still hear Brother Mark saying repeatedly, "God does not want satisfied customers; God wants true friends." In real friendship your friend has to let you know step-by-step who he or she really is deep down. You also have to learn to be real and honest about yourself with your friend.

In Paul's words to the church at Thessalonica we get a sense of the friendship these people shared with one another as Christians: "So deeply do we care for you that we are determined to share with you not only the gospel of God but also our own selves, because you have become very dear to us" (1 Thess. 2:8). Genuine life—life as God intends it to be—has to do with sharing our very selves with one another, the essence of friendship. Perhaps we feel no need so deep within us as the need to be known and to truly know others. To know God and to be known by God is also the essence of prayer. You may yearn for this kind of friendship, this kind of intimacy in your own life. Real friends are hard to find, but God has created us all for genuine friendship.

Prayer Reveals the Real God

Prayer is real, therefore, when the real God meets the real you in real life. Multiple implications spill out of this simple statement.

Who is the real God? People often live with distorted ideas of God. Some of us never discard the simplistic images of our childhood. Many regard God as remote or aloof. Some hold a legalistic concept of God, imagining God looking over their shoulder to catch them in any evil word or deed. Our experience of parental care as children forms the earliest concept of God in our mind and heart. For those who have suffered abuse in the home, a twisted or distorted image of God may color every aspect of life, making it difficult if not impossible to trust anything or anyone. Jesus reveals a portrait of God that stands in opposition to these distorted images.

Jesus said, "Whoever has seen me has seen the Father" (John 14:9). The real God is revealed to us in the person of Jesus Christ. Ironically, as Christians, instead of looking at Jesus to learn about God and how to commune with God, we often project onto Jesus our own ideas about who God is. But, as Bishop Stephen Neill once said, "If when in Jesus Christ we see God, then any previous notion we may have had about God must undergo a reconstruction from the foundation to the roof."

Jesus has been the window to God for a myriad of witnesses. Blaise Pascal, the amazing mathematician and theologian of seventeenth-century France, came to know who God was in the face of Jesus Christ. He was reading the seventeenth chapter of John's Gospel, Jesus' High Priestly Prayer, and pondering who it was who prayed these words of compassion, unity, and love. At half past ten he experienced a quite unexpected self-disclosure from God and was overwhelmed by God's love. Pascal immediately took up his pen and in a frantic hand wrote the words "God of Abraham, God of Isaac, God of Jacob, not of the philosophers and scholars. Certitude. Certitude. Feeling. Joy. Peace. God of Jesus Christ. My God and thy God." His life was never the same again. He resolved to retain this revelation in his heart and mind. He sewed the paper into the lining of the jacket he always wore. It was discovered there when he died.[2]

Knowing about God and knowing God represent vastly different experiences. Pascal was catapulted into a new relationship with God as he came to know God in Jesus Christ. If you wish to know God as God actually is, then fix your eyes upon Jesus. Certainly that focus requires a lifelong quest. You begin a journey into the scriptural witness that is not without its complications. But when all is said and done, I believe that nothing reveals the God of Jesus more clearly to us than his own life of prayer.

Jesus prayed in a startlingly new way. Perhaps that explains why his disciples asked him to teach them how to do it. The unprecedented center of Jesus' prayer can be encapsulated in one word from his mother tongue, *Abba*. This word was not the standard Aramaic term for "father" but a child's very first, most affectionate name for the parent. This single word discloses several important aspects of God's true identity.

Jesus' use of *Abba* reveals a God in whom we can trust. Jesus lived with a certitude about God's steadfast love and presence. "Father, I thank you for having heard me," Jesus prayed at the raising of Lazarus from the dead. "I knew that you always hear me" (John 11:41-42). Indeed Jesus' own confidence in praying led to courage in living. This certainty enabled him to persevere when darkness seemed to engulf him on every side.

The term *Abba* further reveals a God who desires intimacy, who is "for ever close." Despite the paradoxical tension in our minds between a God who is utterly transcendent ("wholly other," the awesome Creator of all that is, totally separate from and beyond the created world) and immanent (closer to each of us in power and love than our very breath), Jesus demonstrated time and time again that this God seeks to be our most intimate friend. It is incomprehensible, but we see this message clearly in the life of Jesus.

Addressing Abba reveals a God who is, in the words of Charles Wesley, "pure universal love." Like the sun, God radiates love incessantly. God surrounds us with the heat and the light of this love. The wooing activity of God suffuses our entire existence. Just as clouds can block the rays of the sun, doubts, catastrophes, depression, worries can block God's rays of love in our lives, but those rays are there nonetheless. As Paul reminded the church at Rome: "Neither death, nor life, nor angels, nor rulers, nor things present, nor things to come, nor powers, nor height, nor depth, nor anything else in all creation, will be able to separate us from the love of God in Christ Jesus our Lord" (8:38-39). Countless Christians have celebrated this affirmation in song:

> Love divine, all loves excelling,
>   Joy of heaven, to earth come down,
> Fix in us thy humble dwelling,
>   All thy faithful mercies crown!
> Jesu, thou art all compassion,
>   Pure, unbounded love thou art;
> Visit us with thy salvation!
>   Enter every trembling heart.[3]

Prayer is not about encountering an idea; it is about building a relationship with the ultimate, personal reality of the universe—the real God.

Prayer Reveals the Real You

Our encounter with the God we come to know in Christ Jesus transforms our life's purpose. Living in harmony with God's vision of shalom becomes our guiding principle. Knowing God helps us to know who we are, to whom we belong, and what is truly valuable in life. Jesus not only shows us who God is but also reveals to us the true selves we can become in his love.

Two simple principles guide the life of an amazing monastic community in the French village of Taizé. Founded by Brother Roger in the middle of the last century, this ecumenical family lives the parable of community and instills hope in all who visit and pray. The first principle: give yourself to Christ each day. Second: open yourself to all that is human; be really present in the world as it is. The central question you need to ask about yourself is the same question we asked about God. Who is the real you in real life? Brother Mark helped me with this question, and I want to share some of his insights with you.

When God's love in Christ becomes the central reality of your life, you discover who you are on the way to becoming your authentic self in the true humanness that God intends for you. Simply put, you discover that you are a precious child of God. Brother Mark was fond of talking about the "self in three senses." Your three selves, as we might call them, are distinct but not separate from one another. They are, in fact, mysteriously interwoven. First, your present self as it actually is now exists deep within. Next, Brother Mark identified the exterior self—that part you show to the world, your public persona. And finally, the true inner self remains in large measure undisclosed to most, something toward which you are moving, the perfection of God's love as manifested in each unique human life.

The real you, therefore, is a mystery. In prayer, the "mystery who is you" meets the "mystery who is God." The real you miraculously combines your failures and triumphs, your most pathetic shame and deepest longings in life. The key to prayer, then, is radical authenticity, the sincerity of your words and the integrity of your life. Come as you really are. Mean what you say. Attitude and spirit are foundational in the life of prayer. You must put on the whole of your genuine self in prayer, for, as Saint Augustine once observed, God does not listen to our words because God reads our hearts. Prayer is listening and speaking heart to heart.

You will find the road to becoming your true self a steep one. On this pilgrimage—as in Christian's journey in *The Pilgrim's Progress*—you encounter many obstacles both outside and within. While movement toward the goal requires tremendous discipline—including the preeminent discipline of prayer—liberation lies ahead. Far from self-indulgence or narcissistic self-actualization, Christian maturity is not so much a matter of "working on yourself" as it is growing in true love toward God and toward others. As a Benedictine monk told me on one occasion, "We only become our true selves when we are wholly turned toward another."

Prayer and the Reign of God

That last statement expresses in another way the truth that prayer—and particularly this quest for the authentic self—is inextricably bound up with the reign of God. Life is relationship, and we cultivate our life in Christ most fully in a Christian community set on a particular trajectory. Through the Spirit, we place our prayers and desires, our efforts and our lives, into the hands of God. In this surrender of ourselves to God's purposes we become potential instruments in the establishment of God's peaceable reign.

We pray, "Thy kingdom come, thy will be done on earth as it is in heaven." In praying this prayer we commit ourselves to offer God's love to all and to oppose injustice wherever we find it. Our path leads to growth in prayer when we honor God's name by waging peace and living in solidarity with those who are broken and alone. We come near to God's reign through our active love, and we need to be close to God in order to be God's agents of shalom, of peace, wholeness, justice, and well-being in the world God loves.

We grow, miraculously, by permitting ourselves to be loved by God in Christ. Abiding in Christ changes us. Friendship with God transforms us. This is the nature of prayer. Paul admonishes us to "grow up in every way into [Christ]" so that our true inner self might emerge, "to maturity, to the measure of the full stature of Christ" (Eph. 4:15, 13).

Hymn

Love Divine, All Loves Excelling

Love divine, all loves excelling,
Joy of heaven, to earth come down,
Fix in us thy humble dwelling,
All thy faithful mercies crown!
Jesu, thou art all compassion,
Pure, unbounded love thou art;
Visit us with thy salvation!
Enter every trembling heart.

Come, almighty to deliver,
Let us all thy grace receive;
Suddenly return, and never,
Never more thy temples leave.
Thee we would be always blessing,
Serve thee as thy hosts above,
Pray, and praise thee without ceasing,
Glory in thy perfect love.

Finish then thy new creation,
Pure and spotless let us be;
Let us see thy great salvation
Perfectly restored in thee;
Changed from glory into glory,
Till in heaven we take our place,
Till we cast our crowns before thee,
Lost in wonder, love, and praise.[4]

Meditation

GOOD NEWS

Lord, help me to keep still
and hold in my heart your words:
"I am with you always."
Help me to care for people.
Help me, now and in the future,
to bring others to God and God's reign.
I know you love me, and you love the world.
But more than that, you yourself are love.
God, you always radiate love, as the sun radiates heat.
Clouds hide the sun, but the sun is always there.
Our troubles hide you from our eyes,
but your love is always there.
This is the ultimate good news I need to hear
over and over again.
Help me to be able to say with Paul
that nothing can separate us from your love.
You work all things together for good.
Help me to ponder over this truth slowly and deeply.
Holy Spirit, help me now and
in all the years to come.
Amen.

3

Attentive PRAYER

God is our refuge and strength,
  a very present help in trouble.
Therefore we will not fear,
    though the earth should change,
  though the mountains shake in
    the heart of the sea;
though its waters roar and foam,
  though the mountains tremble with its tumult.

There is a river whose streams
    make glad the city of God,
  the holy habitation of the Most High.
God is in the midst of the city;
    it shall not be moved;
  God will help it when the morning dawns.

. . . .

"Be still, and know that I am God!
  I am exalted among the nations,
  I am exalted in the earth."
The LORD of hosts is with us;
  the God of Jacob is our refuge.
—Psalm 46:1-5, 10-11

The reason I speak to them in parables is that "seeing they do not perceive, and hearing they do not listen, nor do they understand." With them

> indeed is fulfilled the prophecy of Isaiah that says:
> "You will indeed listen, but never understand,
> and you will indeed look, but never perceive.
> For this people's heart has grown dull,
> and their ears are hard of hearing,
> and they have shut their eyes;
> so that they might not look with their eyes,
> and listen with their ears,
> and understand with their heart and turn—
> and I would heal them."
> But blessed are your eyes, for they see, and your ears, for they hear. Truly I tell you, many prophets and righteous people longed to see what you see, but did not see it, and to hear what you hear, but did not hear it.—*Matthew 13:13-17*

The first words in *The Rule of St. Benedict* are "listen carefully."[1] The great monastic founder most certainly had in mind a reverent, ready, humble, sensitive listening. He conceived listening as a lifelong process of learning. In a world increasingly enveloped in a cacophony of sounds and unrelenting noise, where silence for many has become a virtual impossibility, I am convinced that the key to the Christian life is listening. If listening is an act, then attentiveness is the complementary disposition of the soul. Prayer helps to cultivate a spirit of attentiveness. The secret to an abundant life—a life characterized by meaning, value, and purpose—is attentiveness to God and to everything else around you. I call this attitude toward life, this habit of the heart, attentive prayer.

Prayer as Listening

I would like to associate with this attitude of prayer the painting by Jean-François Millet titled *The Angelus*. (See Plate 3 in Illustrations.) Of course, you cannot listen with your ears to this magnificent work. You have to "listen" to it with your eyes. You have to attend to it with your heart.

Millet depicts a man and a woman, simple farmers, standing in a field. The man, presumably the husband, stands with bowed head and cap in hand, a posture of reverence. His wife's hands are clasped, her head also bowed, and her weary face quieted. Pausing together as the sun begins to set near the end of a long day of work, they have turned to prayer.

In the distance we can see a church spire; perhaps we can hear the bells ringing the hour. Put aside for this time of prayer are a basket of potatoes at the woman's feet, a wheelbarrow of empty sacks, and a pitchfork standing to the man's side. We notice birds making their homeward flight against clouds touched by twilight.

Millet entitled this painting *The Angelus*, having been inspired by a devotional tradition rooted in his French Catholicism and by his own parents' piety and love of life. While the origins of the Angelus prayers are obscure, the practice was well established by his time. Angelus prayers were recited morning, noon, and night at the sound of the church bells. The final prayers of the day commemorated the incarnation of Christ and God's gift of love to the world.

Millet often had seen his father and mother in the very pose he recorded in this painting. He wanted to remind himself and others of the devout and attentive spirit of the peasants in a rosy twilight's peace. According to tradition, when Millet's agent first saw this work, he exclaimed, "It is the Angelus." "Yes," Millet responded. "Can you hear the bells?"[2]

Listen. Can you hear the bells? When do we stop long enough to really hear anything? To listen closely—to remain attentive through every moment of the day, to fully hear the concerns, cares, and worries of people close to us in life—is difficult to do. But to find the God whom we all are seeking absolutely requires listening. This listening, this mindfulness, this attentiveness, converts listening from a mere sensory function into a living response to life itself. The monastic bell calls us to that realization. I'll never forget talking with my friend Father Odo Recker about the bells at Mount Angel Abbey where we met. "They are 'the voice of God' calling to each of us," he said. "They are a perennial reminder that 'turning to God' is more important than anything else we are doing." Listening is "turning to God." The toll of the bell directs the attention of the world, as well as the monastery, to our need "to attend." It reminds us of our need for God and for one another; it calls us home to an attitude of attentiveness to what is real.

Attentive prayer includes many dimensions but none so important as listening to the Word of God and listening in silence to the Spirit of God.

Listening to the Word of God

I am not sure when I first heard the expression "praying the Word." But praying scripture has become one of the most significant ways to listen in this deeper sense for me. Rediscovering the Bible offers perhaps the most effective means for growing in prayer.

Charles Wesley wrote a hymn intended for early Methodists to sing before reading scripture. It poignantly expresses his trust in God's Word:

> While now thine oracles we read
> With earnest prayer and strong desire,
> O let thy Spirit from thee proceed
> Our souls to waken and inspire,
> Our weakness help, our darkness chase,
> And guide us by the light of grace.

The secret lessons of thy grace
  Transmitted through the Word, repeat,
And train us up in all thy ways
  To make us in thy will complete;
Fulfil thy love's redeeming plan,
And bring us to a perfect man.[3]

In their Anglican tradition, with regard to scripture, the Wesleys were taught to pray: "May I always so hear, read, mark, learn, and inwardly digest thy Word that it may be a savor of life to my soul." "Inwardly digesting" the Word suggests what I mean by praying the Word.

Praying the Word involves moving words of the sacred text from the head to the heart. This ancient practice is constantly in need of rediscovery. Its roots go deep. Before the coming of Christ, the Psalms were the prayer book of Judaism, and they remain the foundation of prayer in our two great families of faith. The people of God have been praying the Word for generations. It probably is not an overstatement to say that the basic form of prayer for Christians always has been meditation on scripture.

To pray the Word in the specific sense we are exploring here means permitting the words of the Bible to form the shape of your praying, permitting God's Word to re-form our interior life in every way. The discipline of praying the Word distinctly differs from the academic study of scripture. Each has its purpose; each yields its own rewards. But praying the Word encourages us to enter into God's amazing story of love, to participate in God and God's purpose for creation, to find our place in the story itself.

Reading God's Love Letters

Praying the Word can take many forms. Saint Augustine once described the scriptures as letters from God about

God's love. They are indeed love letters. One of the simplest ways to pray the Word, therefore, is to read scripture devotionally in the same way you would read any letter or e-mail from a friend or a loved one. Think for a moment about a message you received from someone you longed to hear from. Perhaps you experienced this threefold approach to "digesting" the letter:

1. Pick out the main points. You are anxious to quickly absorb the primary details, the important news, the events of significance.
2. Read the whole slowly. Not only are you concerned about the facts, but you want to have some sense of the "feel" of it all. What is the sense of the letter? What was your friend or loved one feeling?
3. Ponder the expressions. Especially if this is a love letter, you may pause on a single word or a phrase, savor it in your heart, roll it around repeatedly in your mind. You may even commit it to memory and "visit it" throughout the day.

Is this not how you read such a letter? Why not the Bible—love letters from God? The implications are huge. To pray the Word means that from time to time you need to focus on the essential matters. You may want to attend to a particular book, for example, Paul's letter to the Galatians. Certainly, reading through the entirety of the Bible in course, perhaps with a lectionary, holds great value. But you also need daily quiet time, time to ponder God's Word in your heart. Luke tells us that after finally locating her teenage son in the Jerusalem Temple, Mary "treasured all these things in her heart" (2:51). We need to treasure the insights received through the Spirit in a similar way.

Meditating on the Word

Meditation, one of the most important forms of praying the Word, makes the heart glad. It involves spending time with the Lord as a dear friend. A rediscovered and popular form of meditation known as *lectio divina,* literally "divine reading," cultivates deep listening to the God who speaks through the Word. This practice allows the Spirit to shape our response in thought, prayer, and action.

Classically this discipline is conceived in four movements: *lectio* (reading), *oratio* (prayer), *meditatio* (meditation), and *contemplatio* (contemplation). After selecting a passage upon which to meditate, the individual or group moves successively through each step of the process. The key to this practice is to permit the text to read you, instead of your reading the text. Rather than turning scripture into an object to be studied or analyzed, the purpose is to permit the Word of God to examine and restore you. *Lectio* is a marvelous way to rediscover the Living Word.

I want to suggest a simplified version of this meditative technique oriented around the four simple words *proclaim, picture, ponder, practice.* And I want to be very practical in my advice.

PROCLAIM. Select a text for your meditation. The stories and parables of the Gospels, which are rich in imagery, character, and real-life situations, lend themselves extremely well to this form of meditation. Likewise, the Psalms are a natural place to begin. Read the passage. I recommend that you actually read it aloud, because it is important for us, and at some times more than others, to actually hear the Word "proclaimed."

PICTURE. Read the same text through again, this time picturing yourself somewhere in the narrative. With which person do you identify? Where do you find yourself in the drama that is unfolding before your eyes?

PONDER. After a third reading of the text, ponder what these words might mean for you today. What insight have you gained about yourself, God, your neighbor? What significance do you attach to your discoveries given your recent experiences, relationships, concerns?

PRACTICE. Following a final reading of the passage, resolve to translate your experience in the meditation into action. What is God calling you to do with this insight today? What action is required? What words need to be shared with others? What does God require of you to be an ambassador of reconciliation and love throughout the course of the day?

In scripture we are repeatedly reminded that God has an untiring interest in us! By praying the Word we realize once again that God wants to comfort us, that God will never forget us, and that in God's sight we are precious and loved with an everlasting love. When we allow God to nourish us for our journey through scripture, then we are praying the Word. Scripture, prayed with an earnest intent, calls us back to the central purpose of life. The Word heals our brokenness and guards against narrow and small visions of life. Praying the Word connects us with the great cloud of witnesses who worked through their own struggles of faith. It becomes the primary filter through which we learn. It sharpens our listening skills so that we can know/hear the world and ourselves aright. It restores sight to our eyes and hearing to our ears, without which we would live life truly deaf and blind, as the Master told his disciples.

Listening in Silence

Jesus needed, and we need, daily quiet time, if at all possible early in the day. "In the morning, while it was still very dark, he got up and went out to a deserted place, and there he prayed" (Mark 1:35). We need moments of silence in our lives. Speaking for the Lord, the psalmist reminds us: "Be still, and know that I am God!" The importance of silence cannot be exaggerated. Silence creates the space necessary for God to come in. It provides the opportunity for God through the Spirit to penetrate us with God's love. Unless we first receive God's love into ourselves, we really have little love to share with others during the day.

What I am talking about is not much more than sitting, quiet, relaxed, intentionally remembering God's presence and asking the Spirit to assist you in your prayer. Sometimes it helps to "hold yourself quiet in God's presence" by repeating a simple phrase in your mind, such as, "My Lord and my God"; "Jesus my Lord"; "Welcome"; "Come in, Lord Jesus." And then, in the stillness, accept God's love. Perhaps nothing is more difficult in life. But God yearns to share this love with you. Accept God's love.

Silence is not a sanctuary from the noisy business of life. It is not an escape. Rather, silence is a tone of being, a disposition of the soul. Silence represents a place of hospitality where you can say, "God, in this quiet moment I am wholly yours. I want to be with you. I want to listen to you. I want to receive the love you offer me in Christ." It provides a space in which you can actually hear God's call upon your life.

One mature in the ways of prayer once told me, "God speaks, but rarely in full or coherent sentences." Ears do not hear the calling. God's words can seldom be read in full paragraphs. You hear God's voice in the deepest part of yourself, that place where you nurture your deepest longings and desires—the human heart.

Paul says to the Thessalonians, "Study to be quiet" (1 Thess. 4:11, KJV). We need that quiet so that in the silent relaxation of heart and mind we might receive and commune with God. Cultivate an attentive spirit. Listen to God by praying the Word. Immerse yourself in the silent wonder of God, for in the stillness and simplicity of that space, you will encounter the living presence of Love.

Hymn

STILL FOR THY LOVING KINDNESS, LORD

Still for thy loving kindness, Lord,
I in thy temple wait;
I look to find thee in thy Word,
Or at thy table meet.

Here in thine own appointed ways
I wait to learn thy will;
Silent I stand before thy face,
And hear thee say, "Be still!"

"Be still—and know that I am God!"
'Tis all I live to know!
To feel the virtue of thy blood,
And spread its praise below!

I wait my vigour to renew,
Thine image to retrieve,
The veil of outward things pass through,
And gasp in thee to live.

I work; and own the labour vain.
And thus from works I cease;
I strive; and see my fruitless pain
Till God create my peace.

Fruitless, till thou thyself impart,
Must all my efforts prove;
They cannot change a sinful heart,
They cannot purchase love.

I do the things thy laws enjoin,
And then the strife give o'er;
To thee I then the whole resign,
I trust in means no more.

I trust in him who stands between
    The Father's wrath and me:
Jesu, thou great eternal Mean,
    I look for all from thee![4]

Meditation

JESUS' CALL

Lord, help me to listen for your voice.
Help me really to pray.
Help me to pray just as you prayed to God.
I know why you prayed so much and so deeply.
For you told us that,
separated from God, we can do nothing.
I too can do nothing good
unless I keep close to you.
So keep me close to you now and always.
You know me deeply, my mind and my heart.
You called your earliest disciples, first,
to be with you, to abide with you;
and, second, to teach and equip others.
I cannot truly love and help others
unless I abide in you.
Lord, show me how to abide in you
in love and in prayer now and in all my days.
Amen.

4

Responsive PRAYER

Then Jesus said, "There was a man who had two sons. The younger of them said to his father, 'Father, give me the share of the property that will belong to me.' So he divided his property between them. A few days later the younger son gathered all he had and traveled to a distant country, and there he squandered his property in dissolute living. When he had spent everything, a severe famine took place throughout that country, and he began to be in need. So he went and hired himself out to one of the citizens of that country, who sent him to his fields to feed the pigs. He would gladly have filled himself with the pods that the pigs were eating; and no one gave him anything. But when he came to himself he said, 'How many of my father's hired hands have bread enough and to spare, but here I am dying of hunger! I will get up and go to my father, and I will say to him, "Father, I have sinned against heaven and before you; I am no longer worthy to be called your son; treat me like one of your hired hands."' So he set off and went to his father. But while he was still far off, his father saw him and was filled with compassion; he ran and put his arms around him and kissed him. Then the son said to him, 'Father, I have sinned

> against heaven and before you; I am no longer worthy to be called your son.' But the father said to his slaves, 'Quickly, bring out a robe—the best one—and put it on him; put a ring on his finger and sandals on his feet. And get the fatted calf and kill it, and let us eat and celebrate; for this son of mine was dead and is alive again; he was lost and is found!' And they began to celebrate."—*Luke 15:11-24*

Prayer is a response to the prior love of God. Words and actions emerge from the quiet moments spent with God in prayer. The attitude of attentiveness is inextricably bound to the compelling summons to action. The listening calls for a response, actually many different kinds of responses. Once we have heard God's call, whether in that still small voice within or in a life-altering event, we must respond. The various forms of prayer that Christians have developed over the centuries reflect our multiple responses to the voice of God. But before we explore each of them in turn, some reminders.

To Pray as Jesus Prayed

When we look at the life of Jesus we see he was motivated solely by love. Love stood as the foundation, the center, the goal of his prayer. When we see Jesus, we see the true God. When Jesus was teaching, he looked at people. He saw those whom others never saw. He acknowledged their presence and their worth. When he was healing, he simply became an instrument of love. His life was lived out in stark contrast to some of the "religious people" of his day, who prided themselves in the way they prayed. You may remember Jesus' words concerning them in his Sermon on the Mount (Matt. 6:5-15). "Do not be like the hypocrites. . . . Do not heap up empty phrases. . . . Do not be like them." They were enclosed in the law and regulations; inflated with pride; trapped, as it were, like a medieval knight in tight armor. Jesus' words to them were metal-piercing in their sharpness but loving. The trap into which they had fallen was that of mistaking the means for the end of prayer. As we begin to look at forms of prayer, remember that prayer is not an end in itself. A loving relationship with God and the loving embrace of our neighbor are the goals.

Note this significant corollary: to pray as Jesus prayed is to become truly human. Through his life of prayer Jesus demonstrated to us all what it means to be a human being. Jesus really cared for each person. He took responsibility for others. He was a man of courage in the face of seemingly insurmountable odds. Jesus developed his gifts for the benefit of others, not for his own self-cultivation. His basic character, along with all his words and actions, made him a man of prayer and the true image of what human life is meant to be. Jesus offered no "but I am only human" excuse. To be truly human is to be created in the image of God, and then—despite our failures, brokenness, and hopelessness—to have that image restored through Christ in our lives. Our true humanity brings glory to God! Bear these thoughts in mind as we explore the shape of our response to God.

An Outline of Daily Prayer

Brother Mark gave me a recommended outline for daily responsive prayer comprising six actions or movements. He suggested touching upon as many of these aspects of prayer as possible each day at some time. When in the depths of despair, it does not come naturally to give God thanks. When we are caught up in our problems or anxieties, we don't tend to think about the plight of our neighbor. When we feel alone and abandoned, we find it difficult to entrust our lives to God. Conversely, when we are on top of the world, we easily forget God. When we are feeling particularly good about ourselves, our need for forgiveness may not seem compelling.

We must be honest with ourselves in realizing that "where we are" affects our prayer. While our circumstances in life certainly shape our response to God in prayer, prayer can shape our attitudes about what life happens to throw our way. This discovery may be the secret behind Paul's ability to say, "I have learned to be content with whatever I have" (Phil. 4:11). On the one hand, prayer can shatter a false sense of security based upon pride and restore the proper foundation of faith; on the other, prayer can call us back to the dignity and worth of our redeemed humanity and restore our hope in God's loving-kindness.

Brother Mark's mnemonic for the forms of responsive prayer spells out the word *artist.* I love that image. Prayer is an art. It draws on our native capacity to create, to dream, to envision. These six particular responses to God in prayer have stood the test of time: *adoration, repentance, thanksgiving, intercession, self-care,* and *trust.*

Adoration

Our first response to God acknowledges whom we worship. Adoration and praise characterize contemporary "praise and worship." With outstretched hands we worship the one, true God, who is awesome and eternal, beyond the capacity of our minds to conceive. An ancient prayer, the *Te Deum Laudamus,* offered up daily in some Christian traditions, begins:

> We praise you, O God.
> We acclaim you as Lord;

all creation worships you,
Father everlasting.
To you all angels, all the powers of heaven,
cherubim and seraphim, sing in endless praise:
Holy, holy, holy, Lord, God of power and might;
heaven and earth are full of your glory.[1]

In adoration we love God back. We love God for God's self, for God's very being, for God's constancy, for God's radiant joy and everlasting love. We adore the Creator for the magnificent universe that was flung into existence out of nothing. We adore the Son for all he has done for us to win us back to our true selves. We adore the Spirit for the transforming power of God's presence in our lives still. To glorify this glorious God is our first, and perhaps most important, response in prayer.

Repentance

When we contemplate our own lives in relation to this God—or compare them with the life of Christ—our inadequacy, our brokenness, and our fallen condition overwhelm us. Like many great figures of the Bible, we find ourselves falling far short of the mark. Like David, we lament our decisions and the destruction they have left in their wake. Like Peter, we bemoan our betrayal of what we know to be good and true. If we are honest, we inevitably come to the biblical conclusion, "If we say that we have no sin, we deceive ourselves" (1 John 1:8). But our failures don't have to lead us to discouragement.

First, we must acknowledge our sins and not cover them up. Then we must fix our eyes upon Jesus. In our quest for forgiveness, it is important to be definite and precise both in asking for forgiveness and in the quest to become the beautiful person God intends us to be. The process of restoration involves the miracle of repentance, forgiveness, and consequent thanksgiving. Let's explore this healing activity of God in prayer more fully.

The Wesleyan tradition presents repentance as a paramount concern because it strikes at the very heart of salvation. Repentance and forgiveness are central to the Christian view of what it is we need to be saved from and what it is we need to be saved into. With all our talk about "being saved," we often forget what salvation is actually all about. For the Wesleys, salvation is both legal and therapeutic; it relates to both Christ's redemptive work for us and the Spirit's transforming work in us; it revolves around freedom from sin and freedom to love. I have always appreciated this balance in the spiritual life. Repentance, like the threshold of a door, opens the way to our spiritual healing, into our paradise. It is like the first step in a journey that leads us home.

No scripture expresses repentance more poignantly than Jesus' parable of the prodigal in Luke 15. You know the story. The son has requested his inheritance, squandered all he has, and finds himself miserable, alone, starving, dying, lost. Stripped of dignity, value, and identity, the son reaches a critical turning point, expressed in these words: "But when he came to himself." John Wesley is the only theologian I have ever found to define repentance as true self-understanding. And I am certain he takes his definition from Jesus' parable. The prodigal "came to himself." In the depth of his despair, he remembered who he was and to whom he belonged. But that rediscovery was a two-edged sword.

On the one hand, the young man understood too well who he was in that moment. He realized how far he had strayed. He was overcome with a sense of guilt and shame. He understood exactly what it meant to lose the dignity of his sonship. And that discovery—that self-revelation—broke his heart. But on the other hand, he came to himself in the sense of acknowledging the one to whom he belonged, realizing that nothing could ever strip him of his primary and eternal identity. He would always be his father's son, regardless. His repentance was an act of contrition and a reclamation of identity. And so he begins the long journey home with his well-rehearsed greeting of sincere humility and remorse—of hope. More than anything else in his life he longed for the face of the one he loved. Nothing could have prepared him for what he experienced in his father's arms just in sight of his home.

Fouquet, a modern Christian painter, captured that sense of at-one-ment, the experience of forgiveness and restoration, that ensued. (See Plate 4 in Illustrations.) In his *Return of the Prodigal Son*, the winding road has led the son home to his father. The earthen tones of the surrounding landscape seem to envelop parent and child and create an atmosphere of peace and serenity. Fouquet placed the son in the center of the picture. Rebellious youthfulness has given way to childlike dependence and simplicity. It is a child that the father holds in his sturdy, caring arms, in a gentle, comforting, and all-encompassing embrace. The child rests his head upon his father's shoulder, buried deeply there, as a sobbing child might seek comfort from a loving parent. The image of father and son in embrace conveys healing and wholeness. The scene is marked with pathos—a sense of relief, of compassion, of "home." Grace, mercy, and peace abound. This portrait of love captures the essence of Henri Nouwen's insight: "Being the Beloved expresses the core truth of our existence."[2]

Repentance marks our turning to God and our return to our true selves. Forgiveness is a mystery; repentance is the key that unlocks the door to forgiveness.

Thanksgiving

With forgiveness comes real joy. "You did not receive a spirit of slavery to fall back into fear," exclaims Paul, "but you have received a spirit of adoption. When we cry, 'Abba! Father!' it is that very Spirit bearing witness with our spirit that we are children of God" (Rom. 8:15-16). Is this not what we all yearn for most deeply in our lives? Is this not what the prodigal experienced in that moment of return? The knowledge that we are forgiven children of God undergirds true thanksgiving and blessedness in life.

Charles Wesley captured the spirit of this gratitude in a hymn "describing inward religion." Its key phrase is the Johannine "hereby we do know" (1 John 2:3, 5, KJV). In the opening stanza Wesley asks a question; then he confidently demonstrates the answer in the successive stanzas:

> How can we sinners know
> our sins on earth forgiven?
> How can my gracious Savior show
> my name inscribed in heaven?
> What we have felt and seen,
> with confidence we tell,
> and publish to the ends of earth
> the signs infallible.[3]

The signs are unmistakable. Those who place their trust in Christ receive his peace, a peace that is unspeakable and unknown. We are thankful first and foremost for what Jesus Christ has done for us. It is by the Holy Spirit that "we know the things of God" and experience God's power in our lives. And the fruit of the Spirit is "the meek and lowly heart." Thankfulness for the activity of the Spirit in our hearts and lives marks the true Christian. When we have found our true home in God's love, we sing with Wesley:

Exults our rising soul,
disburdened of her load,
and swells unutterably full
of glory and of God.[4]

As we are changed from glory into glory in our homeward journey, repentance, forgiveness, and the consequent gratitude of our hearts are essential touchstones along the way. The true Christian is a thankful child of God, and thanksgiving an essential aspect of prayer.

Intercession

Intercession focuses the rays of God's love, like the heat rays of the sun, on others (Mark 2:1-12). It is a fourth form of prayer critical in Christian discipleship. As we read through the Psalms, we notice that many are actually prayers of intercession for the people of Israel. Jesus instructed his disciples to pray for the lost and for the enemy, and he interceded for others continuously.

Brother Mark likened intercessory prayer to the use of a magnifying glass to focus the light and energy of the sun. Perhaps you have offered spontaneous intercessions for others as a name has come into your mind or a circumstance reminded you of another's need. You can include intercessory prayer in your regular prayer practice as well, setting aside a part of each day or a particular day each week to attend to these needs. If possible, do something concrete as well as pray for those in need. Do not be discouraged if you observe no consequences related to your intercession. Saint Monica prayed for her son, Saint Augustine, for years before he was able to perceive God's loving presence in his life. Michael Ramsey, former archbishop of Canterbury, once commented that "intercession is not your words. Intercession is you." Put yourself in God's hands so that God can use you to help others.

The next chapter will look at the last two forms of prayer, prayer as concern for the self and prayer as an attitude of trust, as they relate closely to unceasing prayer. For the time being, remember in all these forms of prayer to pray in the way you would speak to a dear friend. God is a God of power and glory. But God through Jesus has said, "I prefer you to speak to me as a dear friend and to trust me as a very dear parent." Speak to God and trust God like that. "God has sent the Spirit of his Son into our hearts, crying 'Abba! Father!' So you are no longer a slave but a child, and if a child then also an heir, through God" (Gal. 4:6-7).

NOTE: "Hymn" and "Meditation" for this chapter follow Illustrations section.

Plate 1

The Transfiguration *by Raphael*

PLATE 2

ICON OF THE HOLY TRINITY *by Andrei Rublev*

Plate 3

The Angelus *by Jean-François Millet*

PLATE 4

RETURN OF THE PRODIGAL SON *by Fouquet*

Plate 5

Gethsemane *by He Qi*

PLATE 6

PENTECOST *by Jesus Mafa*

Plate 7

White Crucifixion *by Marc Chagall*

Marc Chagall, French, b. Belarus, 1887–1985, *White Crucifixion*, 1938, oil on canvas, 154.3 x 139.7 cm., Gift of Alfred S. Alschuler. Photography © The Art Institute of Chicago.

Plate 8

Walk to Emmaus *by He Qi*

Hymn

How Can We Sinners Know

How can we sinners know
our sins on earth forgiven?
How can my gracious Saviour show
my name inscribed in heaven?
What we have felt and seen,
with confidence we tell,
and publish to the ends of earth
The signs infallible.

We who in Christ believe
that he for us hath died,
we all his unknown peace receive
and feel his blood applied.
Exults our rising soul,
disburdened of her load,
and swells unutterably full
of glory and of God.

[God's] love surpassing far
The love of all beneath,
We find within our hearts, and dare
The pointless darts of death.
Stronger than death or hell
The mystic power we prove;
And conqu'rors of the world, we dwell
In heaven, who dwell in love.

We by his Spirit prove
And know the things of God,
The things which freely of his love
He hath on us bestowed.
His Spirit to us he gave,
And dwells in us, we know;

The witness in ourselves we have,
And all his fruits we show.

The meek and lowly heart,
That in our Savior was,
To us that Spirit doth impart
and signs us with his cross:
Our nature's turned, our mind
transformed in all its powers,
and both the witnesses are joined,
the Spirit of God with ours.

Whate'er our pardoning Lord
commands, we gladly do,
and guided by [God's] sacred Word
We all [God's] steps pursue.
[God's] glory our design,
We live our God to please;
and rise, with filial fear divine,
to perfect holiness.[5]

Meditation

Our Failures and God's Forgiveness

Lord, you are very close to me.
Lord, I am sometimes discouraged by my failures.
Lord, help me not to be depressed
but to fix my eyes on you.
First, Lord, I see love in you—human and divine.
I watch everything you do,
and see it inspired by love.
I watch you going to Jerusalem
and going to the cross.
It is love that gives you the courage to go there.
Your love liberates us from our failures.
Let me receive more of your love and
the freedom you give.
Next, Lord, I see what a human being should
be like in you.
I see that you really care for
each person you meet.
I see you thinking
how best to encourage others.
I see that you are a man of real prayer.
Help me to learn by the ways you prayed.

Knowing you now as I do, Lord,
I want to talk honestly about myself—
my good points and my failures.
I want to be honest.
I want to tell you all.
I want to do better by your strength.
I thank you for so much
that is good in my life.
I am also filled with remorse
for all the wrong I have done.
I want to be forgiven.
I want to be sure of my forgiveness.

I want to know I have heard your voice,
when you say,
"Your sins are forgiven. Go in peace."
Lord, show me how.
Amen.

5

Unceasing PRAYER

Rejoice always, pray without ceasing, give thanks in all circumstances; for this is the will of God in Christ Jesus for you. . . . The one who calls you is faithful, and he will do this.
—*1 Thessalonians 5:16-18, 24*

Then Jesus told them a parable about their need to pray always and not to lose heart. He said, "In a certain city there was a judge who neither feared God nor had respect for people. In that city there was a widow who kept coming to him and saying, 'Grant me justice against my opponent.' For a while he refused; but later he said to himself, 'Though I have no fear of God and no respect for anyone, yet because this widow keeps bothering me, I will grant her justice, so that she may not wear me out by continually coming.'"—*Luke 18:1-5*

Paul tells us to "pray without ceasing." But what does this mean? Brother Lawrence, in *The Practice of the Presence of God,* demonstrates that prayer is a quiet, continuous conversation with God. Mother Teresa of Calcutta notes that "work does not stop prayer; and prayer does not stop work."[1] A wise man of prayer, reflecting on Paul's admonition, once observed that you cannot pray all the time unless you pray at special times. Times of formal prayer punctuate the life of prayer for Christians. In these moments we direct our hearts and minds explicitly to God, in the same way that we spend special time with friends and those we love. But it is also right to say that all of life is prayer. Since prayer has to do with our relationship with God, it never ends. It is the foundational reality of all that we are and do. While intensive in special times set apart, prayer also pervades every word, act, and thought of every day. We can describe this kind of prayer as habituated practice and sustained posture. Unceasing prayer means both frequently repeated acts of prayer and an ongoing quality of life. With regard to these complementary aspects of "ceaseless prayer," I want to carry us back to prayer related to the self and prayer as trust, respectively.

Self-Care

While it is important to adore God, repent and return home, offer grateful thanks, and intercede for others (forms of prayer encountered in the previous session), your spiritual health demands you not forget about yourself. After all, God loves each individual like a child. God longs to be in a loving relationship with you.

You are important because you are a child of God, a person of inestimable value and worth. Prayer is not an effort to batter the self, to beat it down, to repress, despite the fact that self-denial and self-sacrifice are integral to the Christian life. Rather, prayer molds the self into the true child of God. It restores your true identity. It helps you to find the meaning of your existence in relation to God in Christ Jesus.

The ancient Greeks had a word for the process by which an individual comes to maturity. *Paideia* means "instruction through action." It implies a lifelong process of learning and growth. It assumes a journey. Paul used this word when he commanded Christian parents to bring up their children "in the discipline and instruction of the Lord" (Eph. 6:4). Prayer as *paideia* concerns the fundamental shaping of the "perfect" human being, and for those who are Christians (as chapter 7 will discuss), that means "taking up your cross" and conforming your life to the pattern of Christ.

The Repetition of Formational Disciplines

The formation of the self through *paideia*, then, has to do with the use of specific actions—such as habituated forms of prayer—directed toward our moral and spiritual nurture. Prayer in this sense entails all we do in the community of faith to shape the whole person toward maturity in Christ. Prayer involves discipline. Prayer necessitates discipline. Prayer is discipline. But as noted earlier, the ultimate purpose of discipline is liberation.

Unless you practice a musical instrument, you will never be "free" to release the music in your soul. Likewise, prayer—discipline—is necessary for the holistic formation of your self as a child of God. Unless you pray "ceaselessly," you will never uncover your true self; God's glory will never be able to shine through you fully.

And so Charles Wesley wrote:

> I want a heart to pray,
> To pray and never cease,
> Never to murmur at thy stay,
> Or wish my sufferings less.
> This blessing above all,
> Always to pray I want,
> Out of the deep on thee to call,
> And never, never faint.[2]

If you examine the hymn closely, you'll see Wesley defines the true child of God clearly—the disciplined follower of Christ reshaped into Christ's image. Prayer helps to form "a sober mind" and "a self-renouncing will." It enables the disciple to "take up the consecrated cross." Characteristics of the mature Christian include "a godly fear," "a single, steady aim," a perennial concern to praise God in all things, and "a pure desire that all may learn and glorify [God's] grace." Ultimately the "patient spirit" will be guided into "perfect love." Disciplined prayer shapes character. Habituated practices make you who you are.

The parable Jesus told concerning the persistent widow in Luke 18 reinforces the image of constancy in prayer. Before relating the story in his Gospel, Luke says explicitly that the parable will remind the hearers "about their need to pray always and not to lose heart." Jesus practiced what he preached. The scriptures on which he had been raised, and particularly the Psalms, stressed prayer without ceasing. "I will bless the LORD at all times; his praise shall continually be in my mouth" (Ps. 34:1). Psalm 119 might be titled "The Psalm of Ceaseless Prayer." "My soul is consumed with longing for your ordinances at all times" (v. 20). The psalmist meditates on the Law of God "all day long" (v. 97). "Seven times a day I praise you for your righteous ordinances" (v. 164).

Morning and Evening Prayer

Verse 164, in fact, provided the biblical foundation for the Liturgy of the Hours, a daily cycle of prayer in Christian monasticism. Consisting mainly of the Psalms, biblical canticles, hymns, readings, and historic forms of prayer, this Divine Office (as it is also known) was an attempt to pray without ceasing in community, to fulfill that great command. The Divine Office still offers a means by which

God can shape the soul. The Protestant reformers simplified the eightfold pattern of prayer in the Benedictine tradition, developing services of Morning Prayer and Evening Prayer. As dutiful priests of the Church of England, both John and Charles Wesley prayed these forms of prayer every day of their lives!

The brothers began every morning with the words of Psalm 51 or some other scriptural sentence: "The sacrifices of God are a broken spirit: a broken and a contrite heart, O God, thou wilt not despise" (v. 17, KJV). They confessed their sin and heard the words of absolution. They recited the Lord's Prayer. They proclaimed the majesty and praise of God through biblical and ancient forms of prayer. They exclaimed, "O be joyful in the Lord, all ye lands: serve the Lord with gladness, and come before his presence with a song." They recited the Apostles' Creed. "Grant that this day we fall into no sin," they petitioned the Lord, "neither run into any kind of danger: but that all our doings may be ordered by thy governance, to do always that is righteous in thy sight." And in closing, they received the words of this blessing: "The grace of our Lord Jesus Christ, and the love of God, and the fellowship of the Holy Ghost, be with you all evermore. Amen."[3]

The day closed, every day, with Evening Prayer and its similar pattern that reminded the men who they were and to whom they belonged. Over the course of their lives, John and Charles prayed these words perhaps as many as 150,000 times or more altogether: "Glory be to the Father and to the Son and to the Holy Ghost; as it was in the beginning, is now, and ever shall be, world without end. Amen." Can you imagine the shaping influence of this habitual form of prayer? Echoes from these prayers can be heard in John's sermons and throughout the hymns of his brother Charles.

The Benedictines named this habituated pattern of prayer *opus Dei,* the "work of God." Nothing whatsoever is to be preferred to it. Joan Chittester has described this prayer as the center and centrifuge of life. These formal times of prayer are not designed to take people out of the world to find God; rather, they remind us of God's presence in every aspect of life. If I had to summarize the purpose of the Divine Office, I would say that it draws us out of ourselves in order to form within us a larger vision of life. I must confess that when I first started to frame my day with the recitation of Morning and Evening Prayer, I found it a boring intrusion into my life. It took a lot of willpower to stay with it. But little by little I began to learn. Increasingly I appreciated the regularity. I enjoyed the moments of reflection. The prayers became transforming, reforming. Most importantly, habitual prayer—especially repeated forms of prayer—holds the power to cultivate a consciousness of God in the midst of life. And that is why Benedict says, "We believe that the divine presence is everywhere. . . . But beyond the least doubt we should believe this to be especially true when we celebrate the divine office."[4]

Trust

That assertion leads me to the second aspect of ceaseless prayer: the cultivation of a "sustained posture" in life based on trust. The Te Deum, one of the traditional prayers said daily in the Divine Office, concludes with these words:

> Have mercy on us, Lord, have mercy.
> Lord, show us your love and mercy;
> for we put our trust in you.
> In you, Lord, is our hope:
> and we shall never hope in vain.[5]

Brother Mark told me we ought to end all our prayers with an affirmation of our trust in God. The expression of our trust is the ultimate consequence of all our other praying. Prayer is not only a means to find God but the medium of life with God. To entrust one's life to God is the essential posture of the Christian believer.

Reuel Howe's *Man's Need and God's Action* has taught me more about the Christian life than perhaps any other source. Trust and the self are closely linked. Our sense of trust or mistrust, developed early in our life, determines our sense of self in relation to others and to God. Trust cannot be taught. It must be "awakened" in a person. There can be no question that an infant's trust first awakens in response to the mother's demonstration of trustworthiness. A hungry baby who finds sustenance and relief from hunger at its mother's breast begins to trust the world. If a trustworthy environment is not provided, the consequences can be devastating.

Entrusting Your Life to God

Isaiah reminds the children of Israel about the trustworthiness of the Lord: "Can a woman forget her nursing child, or show no compassion for the child of her womb? Even these may forget, yet I will not forget you" (49:15). "Trust in [the Lord] at all times, O people," instructs the psalmist; "pour out your heart before him; God is a refuge for us" (62:8). He sets the exhortation to unceasing trust in the context of God's protection in the past. God had already awakened trust in the Israelites' hearts; God's trustworthiness is the ground of their confidence for the future. In the final singing of the Hallel, the ritual recitation of Psalms 113–118 during the Passover meal, Jesus proclaimed with his disciples in the Upper Room:

O Israel, trust in the LORD!
He is their help and their shield.
O house of Aaron, trust in the LORD!
He is their help and their shield.
You who fear the LORD, trust in the LORD!
He is their help and their shield. (Ps. 115:9-11)

To pray as Jesus prayed is to entrust our lives to God. Jesus prayed constantly. His entire life was a prayer, but special moments of prayer also punctuated his life—in the synagogue, among his friends, in the cold solitude of an early morning hour, well before dawn, in a garden, right to the end. Jesus never lost heart—despite an agony that you and I will never know—because he had entrusted his life to God.

A work of art by He Qi, a contemporary Christian artist from China, captures Jesus in prayer. (See Plate 5 in Illustrations.) He Qi's amazing use of color makes his paintings unique. I particularly appreciate his depiction of Jesus with the disciples in the garden of Gethsemane. We see Jesus as the man of unceasing prayer. While the disciples surround him, sound asleep, worn out completely by the excitement and mystery of the day, Jesus struggles with God in prayer. The disciples are curled (in upon themselves) in sleep. Jesus is completely open to God. Direct. Connected. Unconfounded. Trusting. His attention is focused. His eyes are fixed upon the one goal. His heart and mind are united in a singular communion with his Father.

Jesus' communion with God—his sense of God's eternal presence and trustworthiness—was a continuous state of soul. This attitude of his heart and will was a sustained posture in life, an abiding awareness of God. Jesus demonstrates to us through his life what it means to practice the presence of God, or as Ignatius Loyola later described, to find God in all things. His heart was strong enough "to bear the whole shattered world in compassion." His strength came from unceasing prayer.

Radically entrusting our life to God entails framing all we are and all we do with the rhythm of repeated relinquishment into the mystery and joy of God's new beginnings. This continuous, joyful abandonment into the arms of a God in whom we can trust constitutes a daring surrender. Carl Jung, in a work titled *Aspects of the Masculine*, suggests that surrender, in fact, is the most significant connection between love and spirituality:

> [Love] demands unconditional trust and expects absolute surrender. Just as nobody but the believer who surrenders . . . wholly to God can partake of divine grace, so love reveals its highest mysteries and its wonder only to those who are capable of unqualified devotion.[6]

Mary, like her son, epitomized this kind of surrender. One simple statement reveals the core of her being, her sustained posture in life: "Here am I, the servant of the Lord; let it be with me according to your word" (Luke 1:38). Like Jesus in the garden, Mary trusted God to do with her as God chose. That kind of surrender could never have been motivated by anything but love. It was a total release of mind and heart to God, a relinquishment of the self into the gracious flow of God's provision and purpose.

Prayer—Jesus' prayer and our prayer—is much like a river. The great Nile is a continuously flowing mass of water, but the river would not exist if it were not for the tributaries that constantly feed the river fresh water daily, hourly, minute by minute. The tributaries are like our special times of prayer: daily devotions in the morning or the evening, daily quiet time, special times of meditation.

We need special times, prayer partners, and friends in the life of prayer. Because of them, the river moves incessantly toward its goal. It is oriented to that one end. The river of life continues to flow and will empty eventually into the immensity of God's love.

Hymn

JESU, MY STRENGTH, MY HOPE

Jesu, my strength, my hope,
On thee I cast my care,
With humble confidence look up,
And know thou hear'st my prayer.
Give me on thee to wait,
Till I can all things do,
On thee almighty to create,
Almighty to renew.

I want a sober mind,
A self-renouncing will
That tramples down and casts behind
The baits of pleasing ill;
A soul inured to pain,
To hardship, grief, and loss,
Bold to take up, firm to sustain
The consecrated cross.

I want a godly fear,
A quick-discerning eye,
That looks to thee when sin is near
And sees the tempter fly;
A spirit still prepared
And armed with jealous care,
Forever standing on its guard,
And watching unto prayer.

I want a heart to pray,
To pray and never cease,
Never to murmur at thy stay,
Or wish my sufferings less.
This blessing above all,
Always to pray I want,

Out of the deep on thee to call,
  And never, never faint.

  I want a true regard
  A single, steady aim,
Unmoved by threat'ning or reward,
  To thee and thy great name;
  A jealous, just concern
  For thine immortal praise;
A pure desire that all may learn
  And glorify thy grace.

  I rest upon thy Word,
  The promise is for me;
My succour, and salvation, Lord,
  Shall surely come from thee.
  But let me still abide,
  Nor from my hope remove,
Till thou my patient spirit guide
  Into thy perfect love.[7]

Meditation

Perseverance in the Spirit

This time you may make—slowly, thoughtfully, deeply—your own meditation. Take plenty of time to remember and realize how close the Lord really is.

Reflect deeply again and again on those words:

> Rejoice always, pray without ceasing, give thanks in all circumstances; for this is the will of God in Christ Jesus for you.
>
> The one who calls you is faithful, and he will do this.

Now, think slowly and talk to the Lord about the steps, one after another, in the unfolding call of God upon your life.

Reflecting further, try to discern what God wants you to do as the next steps in your call.

Repeat to yourself in prayer several times:

> Run with perseverance the race that is set before [me]—looking to Jesus.

6

Corporate WORSHIP

In the year that King Uzziah died, I saw the Lord sitting on a throne, high and lofty; and the hem of his robe filled the temple. Seraphs were in attendance above him; each had six wings: with two they covered their faces, and with two they covered their feet, and with two they flew. And one called to another and said:

> Holy, holy, holy is the LORD of hosts;
> the whole earth is full of his glory.

The pivots on the thresholds shook at the voices of those who called, and the house filled with smoke. And I said: "Woe is me! I am lost, for I am a man of unclean lips, and I live among a people of unclean lips; yet my eyes have seen the King, the LORD of hosts!"

Then one of the seraphs flew to me, holding a live coal that had been taken from the altar with a pair of tongs. The seraph touched my mouth with it and said: "Now that this has touched your lips, your guilt has departed and your sin is blotted out." Then I heard the voice of the Lord saying, "Whom shall I send, and who will go for us?" And I said, "Here am I; send me!"—*Isaiah 6:1-8*

Jesus practiced personal prayer and corporate prayer. He worshiped with his community in the synagogue. He joined in the ritual of the Temple. He shared in the sign-act of a holy meal with his disciples. Despite the foundational nature of each individual's relationship with God, everyone needs a life within the great family of God as well. We need both personal and corporate prayer to become whole. In worship we share a most profound experience of God through corporate prayer. Worship orchestrates our common praise of God (Ps. 150).

An Orchestra of Praise

I had my first formal class in worship as a college student at Valparaiso University. I'll never forget what the professor said as he introduced the course. Because many of us were theology majors, he said, "Most of you will take a lot of classes in biblical studies, church history, theology, and ethics. But when your brief journey in this life comes to an end, you will spend the rest of eternity worshiping God. Nothing is more important than worship."

The editor of *Weavings: A Journal of the Christian Spiritual Life,* John Mogabgab, introduced an issue titled "Where Two or Three Are Gathered" with these poignant words, well worth quoting in full:

> "There are times," observes l'Arche founder Jean Vanier, when "together we discover that we make up a single body, that we belong to each other and that God has called us to be together as a source of life for each other." There is a mysterious purpose to human fellowship that far transcends our usefulness to one another in the quest to satisfy basic human needs. The corporate character of human life is not merely an instrument in the

> service of efficiency and convenience for the individual. Instead, as Jean Vanier suggests, there is an intrinsic creativity concealed in every experience of authentic community. In the tissue of relatedness we may glimpse the womb of humanity, which nourishes the formation of whole human beings.[1]

Christian worship is a form of corporate prayer that molds us into the whole human beings that God intends us to be. In worship "we who are many are one body" (1 Cor. 10:17). God creates genuine community around Word and Table and Font. In authentic worship we become one family, praying to God as one community in spirit and truth (John 4:24). Worship at its most basic level is not about style, technique, or order. In true "spiritual worship," as Paul made so abundantly clear in Romans 12, we gratefully surrender all we are and all we have—a living sacrifice of praise and thanksgiving.

The Work of the People

One word often associated with worship is *liturgy*. The word literally means "the work of the people." This corporate work—this shared labor of love—forms us in praise. In this context it is interesting to note that the word *orthodox* literally means "proper praise." To be orthodox does not mean primarily that you believe the right things; rather, it means that you have learned how to praise God in the right way with the entirety of your life. Nothing could express the purpose of the worshiping community more clearly. Worship shapes us in such a way that we believe in God (faith), desire nothing but God (love), and glorify God by offering our lives fully to Christ (holiness). As we have already seen, worship involves a joyful obedience and a daring surrender.

Søren Kierkegaard, the Danish philosopher and theologian, conceived of liturgy as drama. In his view, most Christians misunderstand the true meaning of worship. If conceived as drama, most people, so Kierkegaard believed, view themselves as the audience, with the clergy and worship leaders onstage, as it were. This misconception leads to passivity, apathy, disengagement. Worship becomes simply a performance of the few, entertainment at worst. Properly conceived, however, the people of God are the actors, with clergy and others providing support in the wings, enabling them to offer up their praises in a united voice to God. God is the audience, the witness to this amazing drama of our common life.

Worship has integrity when the fullness of who we are meets the fullness of who God is. No one can be excluded from this arena of discovery; everyone is important in it. Ideally, the drama mobilizes us to action. It helps us make the connections between our liturgy and our life. It enables us to participate in the reign of God. And worship does this consistently through both the spoken word (what we say) and the acted sign (what we do).

The pattern of liturgy we have inherited as Christians from Judaism engages us in all those aspects of the spiritual life that are necessary to an ever-growing relationship with God and neighbor. We see this biblical pattern laid out most clearly in the great prophet Isaiah's encounter with the living God in the context of worship in the Temple (Isa. 6:1-8). I will call it the Isaiah motif. Notice the parallels here with the forms of personal prayer we looked at in the previous two chapters.

Corporate Adoration

The scene opens with an almost overwhelming sense of awe, majesty, and wonder. God is pictured on "a throne, high and lofty." The hem of God's robe fills the entire temple. Angelic creatures whirl about in the air and cry out:

> Holy, holy, holy is the LORD of hosts:
> the whole earth is full of his glory.

The overwhelming presence of the living God causes the foundations of the Temple to shake, and "the house filled with smoke." In the Temple Isaiah encountered a God worthy of worship. God's holiness was, in fact, more than he could take.

Rudolf Otto, in his classic work *The Idea of the Holy,* aptly employed the term *numinous* as he sought to describe this majesty of God. He called God's holiness *mysterium tremendum et fascinans,* both a "tremendous or awesome mystery" that was, at the same time, a "magnetic fascination."[2] God's holiness repels us and it draws us. Isaiah's encounter with God went beyond the rational and ethical elements of religion. For many people, as J. B. Phillips reminded us, "God is too small."[3] Worship introduces us repeatedly to a God who is big enough for our needs, big enough to account for life, big enough to command our respect and worship. Corporate worship, like private prayer, begins in adoration.

Confession of Sin

The prophet can only respond: "Woe is me! I am lost, for I am a man of unclean lips, and I live among a people of unclean lips; yet my eyes have seen the King, the LORD of hosts!" The fisherman Simon Peter shared this same response when he encountered the living God. Undoubtedly, you remember the scene. Simon had been fishing throughout the night and had caught nothing. Jesus borrowed his boat to speak to the large crowd that had gathered on the shore of the lake of Gennesaret. But when he concluded his teaching he told Simon to put out into deeper water and let down his nets. Simon obeyed, and when the fishermen laid out their nets, they caught so many fish the boat was nearly swamped. "When Simon Peter saw it," says Luke, "he fell down at Jesus' knees, saying, 'Go away from me, Lord, for I am a sinful man!'" (5:8). Little wonder that after they brought their boats to shore, Peter and the sons of Zebedee left everything and followed Jesus.

Worship helps us maintain the proper perspective with regard to our relationship with God. Most importantly, it holds us accountable for our sin. In the eucharistic liturgy, as a community we confess our sin in these or similar words:

> Merciful God,
> we confess that we have not loved you with our
> whole heart.
> We have failed to be an obedient church.
> We have not done your will,
> we have broken your law,
> we have rebelled against your love,
> we have not loved our neighbors,
> and we have not heard the cry of the needy.
> Forgive us, we pray.
> Free us for joyful obedience,
> through Jesus Christ our Lord. Amen.[4]

Liturgy brings us into an awareness of the holy. Healing becomes possible only when we acknowledge our brokenness and confess.

We all come as seekers into the presence of God in worship. We long to be healed, to be fed, to be restored. We come seeking Christ. Charles Wesley expressed it well in a hymn:

> See, Jesu, thy disciples see,
> The promised blessing give!

Met in thy name, we look to thee,
    Expecting to receive.

. . . .

With us thou art assembled here,
    But Oh! thyself reveal!
Son of the living God, appear!
    Let us thy presence feel.

Breathe on us, Lord, in this our day,
    And these dry bones shall live;
Speak peace into our hearts, and say,
    "The Holy Ghost receive!"[5]

Forgiveness

God responds immediately to Isaiah's cry of desolation. Through the seraph and a painful yet powerful act of cleansing, God declares: "Your guilt has departed and your sin is blotted out." Henri Nouwen described forgiveness as the name of love in a wounded world. Only love can refashion our distorted selves and breathe new life into our broken communities. Only love can overcome evil without resorting to evil means. Our global community still struggles to learn this evasive lesson in life.

Forgiveness liberates us from our enslavement to sin through the power of God's love in Jesus Christ. It points to unconditional love, which freely gives without strings attached. It is a gift that only God can give us. Paul interceded on behalf of the Christian community in Ephesus that they might experience this treasure:

> I pray that, according to the riches of his glory, he may grant that you may be strengthened in your inner being with power through his Spirit, and that Christ may dwell in your hearts through faith, as you are being rooted and grounded in love. I pray

> that you may have the power to comprehend, with all the saints, what is the breadth and length and height and depth, and to know the love of Christ that surpasses knowledge, so that you may be filled with all the fullness of God. (Eph. 3:16-19)

When we—as individuals and as communities—experience this forgiving love of God, it liberates us and puts the song of freedom in our hearts:

> Long my imprisoned spirit lay,
>   Fast bound in sin and nature's night.
> Thine eye diffused a quick'ning ray;
>   I woke; the dungeon flamed with light.
> My chains fell off, my heart was free,
> I rose, went forth, and followed thee.[6]

Liturgy offers us God's promise of forgiveness. When we hear the words "In the name of Jesus Christ, you are forgiven," and repeat them to one another, God's grace enters our broken lives and makes reconciliation possible. Forgiveness and reconciliation lay the foundation of our freedom in Christ. Reconciliation liberates the human spirit.

Christianity on the African continent, where people have suffered tremendous oppression and degradation, offers a compelling testimony to the freedom that is ours through the Spirit of Christ. In Cameroon, Christian communities have developed a collective art form called Jesus Mafa. Paintings based on local depiction of New Testament stories result in a uniquely African idiom. The Jesus Mafa image of Pentecost powerfully represents the descent of the Holy Spirit in that first worship experience of the Christian church. (See Plate 6 in Illustrations.) It visually reminds us of the bond of fellowship uniting all Christians, not only in our brokenness but also in the gift of the Holy Spirit to each beloved child of God. Young and old, men and women, form a new community. They are ecstatic in joy. Empowered to serve. Set in motion. Uninhibited. Liberated. They dance the praises of the God who forgives and makes all things new. Whenever we gather to worship God in the community of faith, this freedom—an essential of the Christian life—is offered to us anew.

Proclamation

Having experienced the awe of God's presence and the liberation of God's forgiveness, Isaiah next hears the voice of the Lord. While it comes to him in the form of a question, it is proclamation nonetheless. The prologue to the Gospel of John tells us: "In the beginning was the Word, and the Word was with God, and the Word was God. He was in the beginning with God. All things came into being through him, and without him not one thing came into being" (1:1-3). In the great Creation narrative of Genesis, God spoke all creation into existence. Word is tremendously significant. God's speech creates. God's Word gives life.

Words, therefore, have always held a central place in worship. We have already discovered the importance of "praying the Word" as a personal discipline of prayer. Nothing helps us to remember more than the Word in the context of Christian worship.

The roots of this understanding of scripture's function may go back to the Exile when the Hebrews' established the synagogue. While in exile, maintaining their identity in a strange land became critical for the Hebrews. They created place and time to proclaim and hear the Word. And the Word continues to help us in this regard. We read the Word together and remember the stories and the Story of God's amazing love. We reflect upon the great actors in the drama of faith and find our own place within the story. We rejoice in the discoveries, singing our song, as it were, in a strange land. We find ourselves renewed by the transforming power of God's Word in the life of our community. Liturgy interprets anew God's Word for us today. Spiritual growth and guidance are possible only when our eyes, our very lives, are open to the light.

Dedication

Finally, in response to the Lord's question "Whom shall I send, and who will go for us?" Isaiah responds by saying, "Here am I; send me!" Those words must have been reverberating in Mary's ears when she responded in similar fashion to the claim of God upon her life and was called into a ministry she could never have foreseen. Liturgy commissions the people of God and enables us to reaffirm our true vocation. Feeding on the Word and feasting upon the Bread of Life sustain us in our mission to God's world.

"To Sing Is to Pray Twice"

At the beginning of the second century, a Roman governor found it necessary to examine with greater scrutiny the revolutionary developments surrounding Christianity. During the interrogation of Christians he discovered that one of their distinctive practices was to sing a hymn to Christ as to a god. Singing had taken on such a key role in Christian assemblies that this pagan observer felt obliged to mention it in his official report to the emperor. The followers of Jesus continued to sing the Psalms, which were at the heart of the Temple liturgy and synagogue worship. They discovered that singing inspired by the Holy Spirit broke down barriers. To glorify God in song was to join their voices to a cosmic current of praise. Little wonder that Saint Augustine is purported to have said, "To sing is to pray twice."

It may sound radical, but I am convinced that as we sing the music of our faith, we recover the image of God impressed upon our being. Our lives begin to resonate with the song of life God has embedded throughout the universe. Spiritual songs shape and express our calling as the children of God. They enable us to glorify God and give expression to the deepest yearnings of the human heart. They enable us to sing more fully with the accent of God's love. Entering faithfully into the song of the community allows us to understand God's intention more fervently. We become the family of God, living together in praise and in joyful service.

Fred Pratt Green, one of the most gifted contemporary hymn writers, gives lyric expression to these thoughts. I close with his words. If you know the hymn, sing it to the usual tune setting of Engelberg!

> When, in our music, God is glorified,
> And adoration leaves no room for pride,
> It is as though the whole creation cried:
> Alleluia!
>
> How often, making music, we have found
> A new dimension in the world of sound,
> As worship moved us to a more profound
> Alleluia!
>
> So has the Church, in liturgy and song,
> In faith and love, through centuries of wrong,
> Borne witness to the truth in every tongue:
> Alleluia!
>
> And did not Jesus sing a Psalm that night
> When utmost evil strove against the Light?
> Then let us sing, for whom he won the fight:
> Alleluia!

Let every instrument be tuned for praise!
Let all rejoice who have a voice to raise!
And may God give us faith to sing always
Alleluia![7]

Words: Fred Pratt Green © 1972 Hope Publishing Co., Carol Stream, IL 60188.

Hymn

See, Jesu, Thy Disciples See

See, Jesu, thy disciples see,
The promised blessing give!
Met in thy name, we look to thee,
Expecting to receive.

Thee we expect, our faithful Lord,
Who in thy name are joined;
We wait, according to thy word,
Thee in the midst to find.

With us thou art assembled here,
But Oh! thyself reveal!
Son of the living God, appear!
Let us thy presence feel.

Breathe on us, Lord, in this our day,
And these dry bones shall live;
Speak peace into our hearts, and say,
"The Holy Ghost receive!"

Whom now we seek, O may we meet!
Jesus, the crucified,
Show us thy bleeding hands and feet,
Thou who for us hast died.

Cause us the record to receive!
Speak, and the tokens show:
"O be not faithless, but believe
In me who died for you!"[8]

Meditation

NO SUCH THING AS SOLITARY CHRISTIANS

Lord, you remain very close to me.
Serving you is my greatest joy.
I say with a heart filled with gratitude,
"I thank you, God, whom I worship."
I am going to spend plenty of time now
thanking you for many people and many things:
So many faithful ones have shaped me
to be the person I am today.
I pray carefully and lovingly for my family . . .
I pray for my many friends . . .
I pray for members of my community of faith . . .
I pray for others who are now on my heart . . .
I am going to pray deeply and regularly
for these dear ones in my life.
Lord, help me to persevere in
this caring and praying.
Help me to run the race set before me.
I can do this in the grace of the Holy Spirit,
for the Holy Spirit is the spirit of courage,
the spirit of power, the spirit of love.
Holy Spirit, guide and strengthen me now
and all my days.
Amen.

7

PRAYER *as* SOLIDARITY *in Suffering*

He was despised and rejected by others;
 a man of suffering and acquainted with
  infirmity;
and as one from whom others hide their faces
 he was despised, and we held him of
  no account.

Surely he has borne our infirmities
 and carried our diseases;
yet we accounted him stricken,
 struck down by God, and afflicted.
But he was wounded for our transgressions,
 crushed for our iniquities;
upon him was the punishment that made us
  whole,
 and by his bruises we are healed.
All we like sheep have gone astray;
 we have all turned to our own way,
and the LORD has laid on him
 the iniquity of us all.

He was oppressed, and he was afflicted,
 yet he did not open his mouth;
like a lamb that is led to the slaughter,

and like a sheep that before its shearers
is silent,
so he did not open his mouth.
By a perversion of justice he was taken away.
Who could have imagined his future?—*Isaiah 53:3-8*

Then he said to them all, "If any want to become my followers, let them deny themselves and take up their cross daily and follow me. For those who want to save their life will lose it, and those who lose their life for my sake will save it."—*Luke 9:23-24*

We come inevitably to the cross of Christ. I say "inevitably" because this is the extent to which God's unconditional love will always go. In one of the most powerful hymns that Charles Wesley ever wrote, we encounter what J. Ernest Rattenbury described as "a Protestant Crucifix."[1] The hymn lyrically depicts Christ on the cross. Through the power of his words, and the Spirit that inspired them, Wesley draws us into the sights and sounds of that awe-full Friday afternoon:

Endless scenes of wonder rise
With that mysterious tree,
Crucified before our eyes
Where we our Maker see:
Jesus, Lord, what hast Thou done?
Publish we the death Divine,
Stop, and gaze, and fall, and own
Was never love like Thine!

Never love nor sorrow was
Like that my Jesus show'd;
See Him stretch'd on yonder cross,
And crush'd beneath our load!

Now discern the Deity,
Now His heavenly birth declare;
Faith cries out, 'Tis He, 'tis He,
My God, that suffers there![2]

The Mystery of the Cross

As we approach the cross together—stop and gaze and fall and own, as Wesley sings—I want to be profoundly honest. I feel unequal to the task contemplated here. We approach one of the greatest mysteries of life. On one level, only images, poetry, song, and art suffice as we explore the simple statement, "Faith cries out, 'Tis He, 'tis He, my God, that suffers there!" Words seem totally inadequate. Thought spills over into adoration. My greatest hope is that you will experience—although perhaps never be able to articulate fully—what Wesley sang in a later stanza of the hymn:

O, my God, He dies for me,
I feel the mortal smart!
See Him hanging on the tree—
A sight that breaks my heart!
O that all to Thee might turn!
Sinners, ye may love Him too;
Look on Him ye pierced, and mourn
For One who bled for *you*.[3]

Before we even take another step forward, take a moment to stop and gaze.

You have an opportunity right now not just to read another devotional book but to meet the God of love in the face of Jesus Christ in a simple act of prayer. Own the fact that God loves you with the kind of self-sacrificing love you see in Jesus. Allow the vision of Christ on the cross to "break your heart." You have come a long, long way to stand here at the foot of the cross. Invite the Holy Spirit into your broken heart to heal and cleanse, to restore and renew, for God longs for you to be a lover throughout your life, just as Jesus has loved you.

In this chapter we will explore the theme of prayer as solidarity in suffering. My guess is that you will not find too many how-to books on prayer that devote a lot of energy to this topic. But I believe the cross, the central symbol of our faith, draws us immediately into this great mystery. Far from answering questions about it (let alone attempting to solve it!), I simply want us to "live in it" for a moment—as we have just contemplated the cross of Christ—and then see how we might respond in an attitude of prayer. We begin with a disturbing image.

Prayer and Tragedy in Life

Once in a lifetime, if they are lucky, artists turn out a work of art coming from so deep within the heart that it "delivers their soul." For Marc Chagall, that painting was *White Crucifixion,* created in 1938 in the midst of the Nazi terror by this Russian-born French Jew. (See Plate 7 in Illustrations.) When I was determining which work of art to meditate upon in this most difficult chapter, I shared several selections with friends. The possibilities ran the gamut from the Crucifixion altarpiece by Grünewald to Rubens's *Lamentation.* But to a person, when I named the theme of prayer as solidarity in suffering, each said, "Chagall." *White Crucifixion*—disturbing, enigmatic, unsettling—is "ugly" and leaves the impression that suffering surrounds us in life.

The roughly square painting depicts a somewhat distorted Christ, impaled not on the usual Christian cruciform but on a truncated, T-shaped cross. He is clad not in the traditional loincloth but in a Jewish prayer shawl. From above, a blistering white beam of light bathes the cross. On all sides we see frenetic activity. The Red Army marches and attacks. A synagogue and village burn. Homes are destroyed. The world is turned upside down. A man carries away the holy scroll of the Torah. People flee in a boat. Jewish elders floating above cover their eyes in dismay at the horrors below. Disturbing bursts of color intrude upon the white and gray tones that dominate the painting. Pain, agony, and suffering encircle the cross. However one interprets the more enigmatic aspects of this great work, one experiences the painting as immensely tragic.

In recent years we have become all too acquainted with the tragic in life. We can no longer escape it! If we are honest, we come to realize that something is fundamentally wrong. We are all wounded people. Children are abused. Marriages fail. Hearts are scarred by cruelty and exploitation. Woundedness is, unfortunately, a fact of life in this world. We intuitively sense a yawning gulf between the world as it is and the world as God intends it to be.

As we stand in the face of this reality, the good news is that God already has traversed the chasm. God already has acted to ameliorate this suffering. God responded by entering our broken world in the vulnerability of a newborn child. Love came down and dwelt among us, "full of grace and truth," and Jesus never lost that sense of vulnerability. The suffering that surrounded him in life—and surrounds him still on Chagall's cross—penetrated to the very core of his being. But this story of incarnate, vulnerable love, in-fleshed in the person of Jesus of Nazareth, began long before his birth.

The Suffering Servant of God

The "Fourth Servant Song" of the prophet Isaiah (Isa. 52:13–53:12) astonishes most people because this account written several centuries before Jesus' crucifixion so strikingly parallels Christ's suffering. The excessive evil that overwhelms Isaiah's figure of the servant of God leaves him condemned and rejected by all. Despite the cruel abandonment he endures, the servant condemns no one and issues no complaint. Through his silence he remains free and the only one untouched by violence in his inner spirit. He is utter patience. His peace and his expectant waiting upon God undo the knot of our complicity with evil. "By his bruises we are healed." Jesus is the Wounded One of God.

This servant image—and its realization in the crucified Christ—reveals to us a God who attempts neither to coerce us into love nor to impose love upon us. Christ becomes vulnerable. He exposes himself to incomprehension as he dies, at the mercy of those he seeks to love. Through the sacrifice of his life upon the cross, he frees us from the fears that paralyze us. He defeats the enemy of light and life. By living out his life from beginning to end in solidarity with all who suffer, he awakens that which is most noble within each of us. Isaiah's portrait of the Suffering Servant is nothing other than a portrait of "my God, that suffers there!"

The questions Ivan Karamazov wrestles with in *The Brothers Karamazov* by Fyodor Dostoyevsky often fill our own moments of prayer. Can we still trust in God in a world where children are abused? If God is good, how can God permit such suffering in our world? The figure of Job is, of course, the symbol of this enigma. His struggle with God in relation to the personal suffering he endures leads to a startling new insight. It is not an intellectual explanation, a justification of the necessity of suffering, or an attempt to explain the mystery of God's providence and activity in the world. Rather, it is a relinquishment of his life and his tragic circumstances (you fill in the blanks with your own life's story) into the hands of a God who can transform these realities into the instruments of redemption.

Glory in the Cross of Christ

The cross of Christ drove the sharp point of pathos deeper into the human heart than it had ever gone before in human history. The early followers of Jesus ultimately concluded, however, that God was "in it." The crucifixion was "filled with God" not in the sense of a divine fiat from a sadistic wielder of ultimate power but in the sense that "God was in Christ, reconciling the world unto himself" (2 Cor. 5:19, KJV).

When Jesus suffered and died on the cross, God bore the sin and suffering of the world. By giving his life to the bitter end, Jesus shared the fate of all innocent victims of inhumanity. He took the suffering of the world upon himself. He absorbed the agony of broken hearts and twisted lives. Moreover, he carried that suffering into his eternal relationship with the One he called Abba. The definitive response to the question of suffering in our world is the response that Jesus lived out.

For Paul, this identification of Christ with humanity revealed God's glory, long hidden from our eyes. As one well acquainted with suffering himself, Paul was determined only to glory in the cross of Jesus Christ (Gal. 6:14), only to "proclaim Christ crucified" (1 Cor. 1:23), to "know nothing" except this God who absorbed (and absorbs) our wounds into God's very being (1 Cor. 2:2). To the Corinthian church he wrote:

> We do not proclaim ourselves; we proclaim Jesus Christ as Lord and ourselves as your slaves for Jesus' sake. For it is the God who said, "Let light shine out of darkness," who has shone in our hearts to give the light of the knowledge of the glory of God in the face of Jesus Christ. (2 Cor. 4:5-6)

This was the favorite text of my theological mentor, Robert Cushman, and I can hear his often repeated words in my mind to this day: "The only authentic Christian life is a cruciform life." In an "if-it-feels-good-it's-right" world, the glory of the cross makes little sense. But to the hurt, the abused, the wounded, and the lonely, the Savior who identifies with our pain is the light of life. As the followers of Christ we are called to translate, through God's grace, the cognitive dissonance caused by our questions about the brokenness and suffering of the world into resolute action rooted in God's love.

Countless shameful crosses surround us on every side. We all know something of the infinite mass of human tragedy and evil. We are even painfully aware of our own complicity in it all. Moreover, we have sustained wounds of our own that remind us perennially of the power of evil in life.

In Christ, we are invited to participate in a Way that faced the worst, went down into the depths of human misery, and endured the cross before it rose up to proclaim the victory and glory of the gospel of our Lord. The victorious One says to us today:

> If any want to become my followers, let them deny themselves and take up their cross daily and follow me. For those who want to save their life will lose it, and those who lose their life for my sake will save it. (Luke 9:23-24)

What insight does Jesus' cross and his invitation to a cruciform life provide concerning prayer? How do these central affirmations of the Christian faith mobilize us for action? Earlier we explored the notion that intercession is not *our words;* intercession is *ourselves*. Prayer as solidarity in suffering involves compassion and hospitality. These manifestations of our intercession in and for the world are both dispositions and actions.

Compassion

God in Christ "suffers with" the world. This is the actual meaning of the word *compassion*. I believe nothing expresses the central truth of God's essence more fully than compassion, the outworking of God's self-giving love. We see compassion in the cross. Compassion, as one has written, is "the fertile suffering of love that births a new creation."

Certainly none of Jesus' stories proclaimed this imperative more directly than his parable of the good Samaritan (Luke 10:25-37). The parable actually begins with the lawyer's question of the Master, "And who is my neighbor?" The question places the lawyer in the center of his world. It asks of Jesus, "Who around me is worthy of my concern?" This self-centered posture triggers Jesus' response in the form of the story. We know it well. As others pass by, only the Samaritan, the despised and suspected outsider, has compassion on his wounded neighbor. The sting of the parable comes in Jesus' reversal of the original question. "Which of these three," Jesus asks, "do you think, was a neighbor to the man who fell into the hands of the robbers?"

You see, Jesus teaches us not to define ourselves on the basis of where *we* stand but to redefine who we are by our action, by our relationship to those who surround us in life. "Demonstrate through your life," he says in essence, "what a true neighbor should be like. Have compassion. 'Suffer with' those who lie wounded around you." My friend and spiritual guide Brother Mark titled a chapter in his book *Love and Life's Journey* "Praying with Eyes Open to the World." If we pray in this posture through our action, we practice compassion.

Hospitality

The other active manifestation of prayer as solidarity in suffering is hospitality. Hospitality concretely expresses the love that binds us to Christ and to one another within the human family. It is a profound response to the crucified One who takes in the whole world by his wide embrace upon the cross. Listening and hospitality share much in common. Both are dispositions, what I have called postures, in life. A poignant statement from *Gleanings*, a significant volume among the writings of Douglas Steere, links these two aspects of our spiritual lives closely: "To 'listen' another's soul into a condition of disclosure and discovery may be almost the greatest service that any human being ever performs for another."[4]

Hospitality creates an opportunity for the one who has no voice to speak. It offers space to another person. It provides a safe place to be honest and real and wounded. It acknowledges the presence of the invisible person. Hospitality breaks down the barriers that separate us from one another. It embraces and welcomes the forgotten, the lonely, and the lost. It opens a way for the wounded to be healed. This prayer of hospitality is challenging because it "listens" another soul into love.

My wife, Janet, had an amazing experience with a child, a homeless little girl being accommodated at our church through Interfaith Hospitality Network. Following an afternoon spent playing together, as Janet prepared to leave for the day, the girl asked her, "I forgot. What was your name?" "My name is Janet," she said. With a joyful twinkle in her eyes, the girl replied, "I will remember that name forever." The cross opens our hearts and affords us the profound privilege to become God's instruments who "pray" our neighbors into healing and abundant life through our actions.

In the spring of 1999 I made my first visit to the Baltic states. I fell in love with the resurrected Christian communities of Lithuania. A local treasure known as the Hill of the Crosses rises on a small mound not far from the city of Siauliai. It stands as a memorial to the suffering of Christians through the years.

For nearly half a century the people of Lithuania suffered under Soviet occupation. Since the socialist state was vehemently atheistic, the occupying forces made every effort to destroy the symbols of religious communities. They particularly targeted the Hill of the Crosses because it stood as an ancient center of Christian veneration and prayer. Three times soldiers removed all the crosses from the hill, but pilgrims to the site repeatedly replaced them under the darkness of night. Finally in 1985, the Soviets left the hill in peace. Since that time, Christians from all over the world have traveled to Siauliai to plant crosses on the hill. All shapes and sizes of crosses reflect the cultures and traditions of Christians they represent. Hundreds of thousands of crosses cover the entire hill today.

I planted my own cross at Siauliai on Good Friday during Holy Week in 1999. It is a perennial reminder to me of the power of solidarity in suffering, a tangible sign of the God who loved us enough to identify with each of us in our suffering. The cross transcends the mystery of evil; our own suffering finds its ultimate explanation in the passion of Christ on the cross. At Siauliai, the locals say breezes blowing through the forest of crosses on windy days produce a uniquely beautiful music.

Hymn

God of Unexampled Grace

God of unexampled grace,
    Redeemer of [us all],
Matter of eternal praise
    We in Thy passion find:
Still our choicest strains we bring,
    Still the joyful theme pursue,
Thee the Friend of sinners sing,
    Whose love is ever new.

Endless scenes of wonder rise
    With that mysterious tree,
Crucified before our eyes
    Where we our Maker see:
Jesus, Lord, what hast Thou done?
    Publish we the death Divine,
Stop, and gaze, and fall, and own
    Was never love like Thine!

Never love nor sorrow was
    Like that my Jesus show'd;
See Him stretch'd on yonder cross,
    And crush'd beneath our load!
Now discern the Deity,
    Now His heavenly birth declare;
Faith cries out, 'Tis He, 'tis He,
    My God, that suffers there!

. . . .

O, my God, He dies for me,
    I feel the mortal smart!
See Him hanging on the tree—
    A sight that breaks my heart!
O that all to Thee might turn!
    Sinners, ye may love Him too;

Look on Him ye pierced, and mourn
For One who bled for you.

Weep o'er your Desire and Hope
With tears of humblest love;
Sing, for Jesus is gone up,
And reigns enthroned above!
Lives our Head, to die no more;
Power is all to Jesus given,
Worshipp'd as He was before,
Th'immortal King of heaven.

Lord, we bless Thee for Thy grace
And truth, which never fail,
Hastening to behold Thy face
Without a dimming veil:
We shall see our heavenly King,
All Thy glorious love proclaim,
Help the angel choirs to sing
Our dear triumphant Lamb.[5]

Meditation

SHARING IN CHRIST'S SUFFERING

Lord, thank you for this special time
set apart to be with you.
Thank you for all the help you are giving me.
I want to be a true disciple.
Like Paul, I want you to be more precious
than all my abilities and achievements.
More important than anything else to me
is a real relationship with you.
I want to know you as a close friend.
That is what I want.
When I live close to you as a true friend,
I feel a new energy, a new joy, a new love,
and that is the power of your resurrection.
Lord, you could not have Easter morning
before the cross of Good Friday.
So in order to have your risen power and joy—
and to share them with others—
I am also ready to give up my own
selfish ambitions and desires.
All I care for is to know you.
Lord, that is true. I mean it.
Amen.

8

The EUCHARISTIC *Meal*

Now on that same day two of them were going to a village called Emmaus, about seven miles from Jerusalem, and talking with each other about all these things that had happened. While they were talking and discussing, Jesus himself came near and went with them, but their eyes were kept from recognizing him. . . .

As they came near the village to which they were going, he walked ahead as if he were going on. But they urged him strongly, saying, "Stay with us, because it is almost evening and the day is now nearly over." So he went in to stay with them. When he was at the table with them, he took bread, blessed and broke it, and gave it to them. Then their eyes were opened, and they recognized him; and he vanished from their sight. They said to each other, "Were not our hearts burning within us while he was talking to us on the road, while he was opening the scriptures to us?" That same hour they got up and returned to Jerusalem; and they found the eleven and their companions gathered

> together. They were saying, "The Lord has risen indeed, and he has appeared to Simon!" Then they told what had happened on the road, and how he had been made known to them in the breaking of the bread.—*Luke 24:13-16, 28-35*

> Day by day, as they spent much time together in the temple, they broke bread at home and ate their food with glad and generous hearts, praising God and having the goodwill of all the people. And day by day the Lord added to their number those who were being saved.—*Acts 2:46-47*

Nothing gives me greater joy than celebrating the sacrament of the Lord's Supper. Of the hundreds of times I have gathered with fellow Christians around the table, one event stands out in my mind. I was teaching a seminary course during the summer. Our class was invited to prepare the final service of worship for the several classes being held concurrently on the campus. Our time together, learning and growing in our faith, had been nothing short of glorious, and we wanted this experience of worship to be a real celebration! Experience had taught me that one of the best ways to create a joyful atmosphere for the celebration of the sacrament was to employ African rhythms and songs because the African church is a singing and dancing community. That is precisely what we did.

Before I consecrated the elements, I invited the community into a new practice. Instead of the bread and the cup being distributed near the table, the usual custom, the elements would be held at the doors. The people were to receive these symbols of God's life and love as they began their journey back out into God's world. The sacramental meal would become food for their continuing pilgrimage into all that lay ahead. I announced that as we processed out together we would sing a joyful African chorus, "Jesus, he is good!" I invited them to let go of their inhibitions, and if the Spirit should set their feet to dancing, not to resist but dance and sing to the glory of God. I prayed the Prayer of Great Thanksgiving, blessing the elements, particularly giving thanks to God for the wonder, the gift of the time we had spent together. And then, oh my goodness, the celebration began. We sang and danced our way out of that chapel into the world, receiving God's nourishment and grace and power to become God's faithful ones yet again. One student ran back to me with tears streaming down her cheeks and said, "Today, for the first time, I experienced the sacrament as Joy!"

In the early church, every Sunday was a "little Easter." Every Lord's Day presented another opportunity to celebrate the fact that Jesus was not dead but alive. "The Lord is risen!" those early disciples proclaimed. "He is risen indeed! Alleluia!" The keynote of worship was thanksgiving and joy. The joy sometimes was so great that it could not be contained. As we conclude this study of being "changed from glory into glory," we consider the eucharistic meal as the most profound form of prayer for the Christian believer.

Praying Around a Table

The sacrament of the Lord's Supper—also known as Eucharist or Holy Communion—is a multidimensional event. Its profundity lies in its simplicity. At its most basic level, the Eucharist is a meal. As a primal symbol, it elicits our deepest feelings about family and community, fellowship and intimacy. We need only bring our hunger and thirst for righteousness; in the meal God nourishes us with all good things necessary for our spiritual health. God uses the material—the common elements of bread and the fruit of the vine—to reveal the spiritual. The sacrament demonstrates to us that God takes the common and the ordinary, even you and me, and invests them with divine significance. It reinforces the knowledge that our God is a God who acts, a loving parent who is eager to be actively involved in our lives, concerned even about our hunger and our thirst.

In *The Imitation of Christ,* Thomas à Kempis observed that we need to be fed from two tables, the table of the holy word and the table of the holy sacrament.[1] The sacrament is the "visible Word," that place in our community life where God's love becomes visible.

The dimensions of time—past, present, and future—offer a helpful framework for thinking about the sacrament of the Lord's Supper. Several of Charles Wesley's hymns express this understanding.

Past: The Lord's Supper

The Lord's Supper (sometimes misnamed the "Last Supper") memorializes the passion of Christ. In it, as Paul says, we "proclaim the Lord's death until he comes" (1 Cor. 11:26). This dimension focuses on *remembrance.* We recall the sacrifice Christ made on the cross on our behalf. As a memorial the meal reconnects us with the *love* of God in the Crucified that sets us free.

> Jesu, suffering Deity,
> Can we help remembering Thee?
> Thee, whose blood for us did flow,
> Thee, who diedst to save Thy foe?
> [Redeemer of all humankind,]
> Gladly now we call to mind,

Thankfully Thy grace approve,
Take the tokens of Thy love.[2]

Present: The Eucharistic Feast

The Eucharist, as we have already seen, is a meal of *thanksgiving*. Many Christians, for various reasons, seem to have fixated on the past and have never moved into this present dimension characterized by grace and joy. Rather than a celebration, their experience of the meal more often resembles a funeral rite. But just as *grace* and *gratitude* are closely linked words, so are *grace* (*charis* in Greek) and *thanksgiving* (in Greek, *eu-charis-tia*). In the Eucharist we celebrate God's mighty acts of salvation, but even more importantly, we commune with a risen and present Lord with thankful, joyful hearts. The meal is both sign and means of this real presence of the Risen One.

Sinner, with awe draw near,
And find thy Saviour here,
In His ordinances still,
Touch His sacramental clothes;
Present in His power to heal,
Virtue from His body flows.

. . . .

Pardon, and power, and peace,
And perfect righteousness
From that sacred Fountain springs;
Wash'd in His all-cleansing blood
Rise, ye worms, to priests and kings,
Rise in Christ, and reign with God.[3]

Future: The Heavenly Banquet

Perhaps we most neglect the future dimension of Holy Communion in our time. Not only is the meal a memorial and a thanksgiving celebration, it is a pledge of heaven and an anticipation of the consummation of all things in Christ. It provides a foretaste of that great heavenly banquet in which the faithful will one day share. It plants a seed of hope in our lives. Whenever we gather around the table, we are never alone. The "great cloud of witnesses"—those who have fought the good fight and run the race with perseverance, our heroes and mentors and loved ones in the faith—surround us and join us in one great act of praise.

> How glorious is the life above,
> Which in this ordinance we taste;
> That fulness of celestial love
> That joy which shall for ever last!
>
> . . . .
>
> Sure pledge of ecstasies unknown
> Shall this Divine communion be;
> The ray shall rise into a sun,
> The drop shall swell into a sea![4]

The Prayer of Great Thanksgiving

All these dimensions of the eucharistic meal come into clear focus in the Prayer of Great Thanksgiving, perhaps the most central prayer of the Christian faith. In this prayer of consecration, which provides a pattern of prayer not unlike the "Our Father," we lift our hearts up to the Lord, remember God's mighty acts in creation and redemption, proclaim God's holiness, give thanks for the gift of new life in Christ, and invite the Holy Spirit to descend upon God's gifts and God's people once again. But at the center of the prayer lies what Dom Gregory Dix calls the fourfold action of the Eucharist, namely, *taking, blessing, breaking,* and *giving.*[5] Each of these actions can potentially shape our life of prayer.

TAKING. Jesus takes into his hands the bread and the wine. The action carries meaning for our everyday lives. Human labor produces the bread. People plant, nurture, and harvest the wheat. They transport it to a mill; they crush and sift grain and send wheat to a bakery. There dough is mixed, then kneaded and baked. The bread is shipped. Vines are cultivated lovingly. Grapes are picked, perhaps by migrant workers living on a minimum wage. The sparkling juice of the fruit is bottled, labeled, and shipped. *Taking* involves a lot of work. "Take my life," we pray in the hymn, "and let it be consecrated all to Thee."[6] Just as Jesus takes the bread and the cup into his hands, he takes our lives and invests them with divine significance.

BLESSING. Whenever faithful Jews offer thanks to Yahweh, they begin with these words: *"Baruch atah Adonai, elohaynu melech haolam."* "Blessed are you, O Lord our God, sovereign of the universe." They thank God first by blessing God. All that we have and all that we are is a blessing from God. We bless God for the wonder of creation; for making us in such a way that our hearts are restless until they find their rest in our Creator; for Jesus, our friend and our brother, whom we long to know and love and follow more intimately every day; for the gift of the Holy Spirit, who comforts and guides; and for the way in which Jesus brought God's reign of Love into the world. What if we were to begin every prayer, like our Jewish brothers and sisters do, "Blessed are you, O Lord our God, sovereign of the universe"?

BREAKING. "The bread that we break," asks Paul, "is it not a sharing in the body of Christ?"(1 Cor. 10:16). In order for the one loaf to be shared, it has to be broken.

The so-called "fraction" in the eucharistic liturgy is one of the most significant moments in the whole rite. Breaking the bread signals an intimate exchange. When we use the expression, as did the earliest Christians, "to break bread together," we refer to a special, a sacred, event. Meals enable us to experience the joy of intimacy with others. Jesus' sharing of his life with us, from beginning to end, is just that intimate. How does the image of breaking relate to our life of prayer? Perhaps it suggests that we open ourselves up in such a way as to become intimate with God. Perhaps it means that we become vulnerable enough with one another that we can actually help one another to discover the true self deep within. Early Christians "broke bread together" and consequently developed "glad and generous hearts."

Jürgen Moltmann is a name synonymous with the "theology of hope." I first met Professor Moltmann when I was a graduate student at Duke University. During one of his visits to campus, I timidly invited him to lunch, and we enjoyed a wonderful meal together. While introducing myself to him more fully, I explained that I was working in my doctoral studies with Frank Baker. "Oh," he interrupted, "I'd like to share a story with you about Frank and Nellie Baker."

During the war a German prisoner of war camp was set up on England's northeast coast. A young pastor and his wife served a small Methodist circuit close by. They were filled with compassion and compelled to do something to reach out to the prisoners. The couple asked the commander for permission to take a prisoner to church each Sunday and then to their home where they would eat Sunday dinner together. It was agreed.

Sunday after Sunday throughout the course of the war, a steady flow of German soldiers worshiped and ate with the Bakers. This world-famous theologian paused, looked at me intently, and said, "One of those soldiers was a young man by the name of Jürgen Moltmann. And I want you to know that the seed of hope was planted in my heart around Frank and Nellie Baker's dinner table." "They broke bread at home," Luke tells us, "and ate their food with glad and generous hearts" (Acts 2:46).

GIVING. In the sacrament, Jesus gives himself to us. He offers all that he is. He lays himself before each of us and says, "I am yours, and you are mine forever." That is his new covenant with us. John Wesley's "Covenant Prayer" outlines what it means for us to "give ourselves to Christ, as he has given himself to us."

> I am no longer my own, but thine.
> Put me to what thou wilt, rank me with whom
> thou wilt.
> Put me to doing, put me to suffering.
> Let me be employed by thee or laid aside for thee,
> exalted for thee or brought low by thee.
> Let me be full, let me be empty.
> Let me have all things, let me have nothing.
> I freely and heartily yield all things
> to thy pleasure and disposal.
> And now, O glorious and blessed God,
> Father, Son, and Holy Spirit,
> thou art mine, and I am thine. So be it.
> And the covenant which I have made on earth,
> let it be ratified in heaven. Amen.[7]

Every time we gather around the table of the Lord, we are shaped by the taking and the blessing, the breaking and the giving. These actions establish another rhythm within our life of prayer and unite us with the risen Lord.

This Holy Mystery

The experience of the Resurrection and the mystery of "this holy meal" come together most profoundly in the story of two disciples on the road to Emmaus. When Jesus "breaks the bread," the disciples' eyes are opened, and they perceive the presence of the risen Christ. Their encounter with the resurrected Lord gives them new eyes with which to see. No longer could their eyes rest on the surface of things. They were able to see into the invisible. They were able to see the world and other people as God sees them. They were able to see the seeds of the Resurrection all around them. For them, in Christ, all things became new. The testimony of the acts of the apostles bears witness to these radical changes and, as Luke tells us, turned the world upside down. The Lord bids us come, come to the table and be filled, be transformed, become real.

> In rapturous bliss
> He bids us do this,
> The joy it imparts
> Hath witness'd His gracious design in our hearts.
>
> . . . .
>
> With bread from above,
> With comfort and love
> Our spirit He fills,
> And all His unspeakable goodness reveals.
>
> O that all men would haste
> To the spiritual feast,
> At Jesus's word
> *Do this,* and be fed with the love of our Lord![8]

We catch just a glimpse of the joy that comes in traveling life's road with the risen Lord by our side in the magnificent depiction of the Emmaus event by He Qi. (See Plate 8 in Illustrations.) We meditated on another work by this Chinese artist when we considered unceasing prayer in chapter 5. Here, Jesus walks with two of his disciples, but the identity of this mysterious companion is hidden from their eyes. He wraps his large arms around them both, and their hearts burn within them.

Prayer is an amazing journey. My ardent hope for you is that your heart burns within you to know Jesus more clearly, love him more dearly, and follow him more nearly. He loves you so.

Hymn

Ah, Tell Us No More

Ah, tell us no more
The spirit and power
Of Jesus our God
Is not to be found in this life-giving food!

Did Jesus ordain
His supper in vain,
And furnish a feast
For none but His earliest servants to taste?

Nay, but this is His will,
(We know it and feel,)
That we should partake
The banquet for all He so freely did make.

In rapturous bliss
He bids us do this,
The joy it imparts
Hath witness'd His gracious design in our hearts.

'Tis God we believe,
Who cannot deceive,
The witness of God
Is present, and speaks in the mystical blood.

Receiving the bread,
On Jesus we feed:
It doth not appear,
His manner of working; but Jesus is here!

With bread from above,
With comfort and love
Our spirit He fills,
And all His unspeakable goodness reveals.

O that [people] would haste
To the spiritual feast,

At Jesus's word
Do this, and be fed with the love of our Lord!

True Light of mankind,
Shine into their mind,
And clearly reveal
Thy perfect and good and acceptable will.

Bring near the glad day
When all shall obey
Thy dying request,
And eat of Thy supper, and lean on Thy breast.

To [humans] impart
One way and one heart,
Thy people be shown
All righteous and spotless and perfect in One.

Then, then let us see
Thy glory, and be
Caught up in the air,
This heavenly supper in heaven to share.[9]

Meditation

BEGINNING ANEW AT THE RESURRECTION MEAL

Risen Lord,
I am overwhelmed by joy
as I sit in your presence.
You are alive and you live for evermore
to teach me, to encourage me,
and to help me find my way home.
I love you, Lord, and I always will.
I am hungry and I need to be fed.
I am thirsty and long to have my thirst quenched.
But I know that you are the bread of life.
You are living water, bursting forth within me,
and if I place my life into your caring hands
I will never again feel the pangs of hunger;
I will never again thirst.
For "the Spirit and the bride say, 'Come.'
And let everyone who is thirsty come.
Let anyone who wishes
take the water of life as a gift."
You offer me the gift of life, O God.
Amen. Come, Lord Jesus!
Amen.

Epilogue

Saint Augustine one time said that true, whole prayer is nothing but love. Being changed from glory into glory is really nothing other than learning to love as God has so graciously loved us in Christ Jesus. Love defines prayer, and prayer helps us to be more loving people. I hope that you come away from this experience with a greater sense of God's love for you and a greater desire to become an instrument of God's love in as many different directions as you can imagine.

Charles Wesley wrote a hymn on prayer, and I leave you with his words as you continue your journey into the deeper mysteries of God's love, changed from glory into glory:

> Jesu, thou sovereign Lord of all,
>   The same through one eternal day,
> Attend thy feeblest followers' call,
>   And Oh! instruct us how to pray!
> Pour out the supplicating grace,
> And stir us up to seek thy face!
>
> We cannot think a gracious thought,
>   We cannot feel a good desire,
> Till thou who call'dst a world from naught
>   The power into our hearts inspire;

And then we in thy Spirit groan,
And then we give thee back thy own.

Jesus, regard the joint complaint
Of all thy tempted followers here,
And now supply the common want,
And send us down the Comforter;
The Spirit of ceaseless prayer impart,
And fix thy Agent in our heart.

To help our soul's infirmity,
To heal thy sin-sick people's care,
To urge our God-commanding plea,
And make our heart a house of prayer,
The promised Intercessor give,
And let us now thyself receive.

Come in thy pleading Spirit down
To us who for thy coming stay;
Of all thy gifts we ask but one—
We ask the constant power to pray;
Indulge us, Lord, in this request!
Thou canst not then deny the rest.[1]

Notes

Introduction

1. Charles Wesley, "Love Divine, All Loves Excelling," in *The Works of John Wesley*, vol. 7, *A Collection of Hymns for the Use of the People Called Methodists*, ed. Franz Hildebrandt, Oliver A. Beckerlegge, and James Dale (Nashville, Tenn.: Abingdon Press, 1983), no. 374.3.

Chapter 1

1. Charles Wesley, *The Unpublished Poetry of Charles Wesley*, vol. 2, *Hymns and Poems on Holy Scripture*, ed. ST Kimbrough Jr. and Oliver A. Beckerlegge (Nashville, Tenn.: Kingswood Books, 1990), 111.

2. German Epilepsy Museum, Kork, "Epilepsy Motifs in the Epilepsymuseum Kork. Raphael," http://www.epilepsiemuseum.de/alt/raffaelen.html.

3. C. Wesley, "Holy Lamb, Who Thee Confess," in *Collection of Hymns*, no. 515.3.

4. Ibid., no. 515.

Chapter 2

1. "Rublev's Trinity Icon," based on G. Vzdornov's article in *An Anthology* (Moscow: Iskusstvo Publications,

1981), 205–12. http://hannover.park.org/Guests/Russia/moscow/sergiev/rublev.html.

2. Emile Cailliet, *Pascal: The Emergence of Genius*, 2nd ed. (New York: Harper Torchbook, 1961), 131.

3. Wesley, "Love Divine, All Loves Excelling," in *Collection of Hymns*, no. 374.1.

4. Ibid., no. 374.

Chapter 3

1. Timothy Fry, ed., *The Rule of St. Benedict in English* (Collegeville, Minn.: Liturgical Press, 1982), 15.

2. "The Angelus: an artistic rendering" The Marian Library / International Marian Research Institute http://www.udayton.edu/mary/gallery/artists/angelus.html.

3. C. Wesley, "Inspirer of the Ancient Seers," in *Collection of Hymns*, no. 87.2, 4.

4. C. Wesley, "Still for Thy Loving Kindness, Lord," in *Collection of Hymns*, no. 89.

Chapter 4

1. Fourth/fifth-century hymn, "Canticle of the Holy Trinity" (*Te Deum Laudamus*), text provided by International Consultation on English Texts, revised by English Language Liturgical Consultation, in *The United Methodist Hymnal* (Nashville, Tenn.: The United Methodist Publishing House, 1989), no. 80.

2. Henri J. M. Nouwen, *Life of the Beloved: Spiritual Living in a Secular World* (New York: Crossroad, 1992), 28.

3. C. Wesley, "How Can We Sinners Know," in *The United Methodist Hymnal*, no. 372, stanzas 1–2.

4. C. Wesley, "How Can a Sinner Know," in *Collection of Hymns*, no. 93.2.

5. Stanza 1: *The United Methodist Hymnal*, no. 372; stanzas 2–6, C. Wesley "How Can a Sinner Know," in *Collection of Hymns*, no. 93.2.

Chapter 5

1. Mother Teresa, *Works of Love Are Works of Peace* (San Francisco: Ignatius Press, 1996), 103.

2. C. Wesley, "Jesu, My Strength, My Hope," in *Collection of Hymns*, no. 292.4.

3. *John Wesley's Sunday Service of the Methodists in North America* (Nashville, Tenn.: The United Methodist Publishing House, 1984), 7, 11, 13, 9.

4. Fry, *Rule of St. Benedict*, 47.

5. "Canticle of the Holy Trinity," in *The United Methodist Hymnal*, no. 80.

6. C. G. Jung, *Aspects of the Masculine*, trans. R. F. C. Hull (Princeton, N.J.: Princeton University Press, 1989), 59.

7. C. Wesley, "Jesu, My Strength, My Hope," in *Collection of Hymns*, no. 292.

Chapter 6

1. John S. Mogabgab, "Editor's Introduction," *Weavings: A Journal of the Christian Spiritual Life*, 5, no. 4 (July/August 1990): 2.

2. See Rudolf Otto, *The Idea of the Holy: An Inquiry into the Nonrational Factor in the Idea of the Divine and Its Relation to the Rational*, trans. John W. Harvey (London: Oxford University Press, 1958).

3. J. B. Phillips, *Your God Is Too Small* (New York: Touchstone Books, 1997).

4. "A Service of Word and Table II," in *The United Methodist Hymnal*, 12.

5. C. Wesley, "See, Jesu, Thy Disciples See," in *Collection of Hymns*, no. 474.1, 3-4.

6. C. Wesley, "And Can It Be, That I Should Gain," in *Collection of Hymns*, no. 193.4.

7. Fred Pratt Green, "Let the People Sing!" in *The Hymns and Ballads of Fred Pratt Green* (Carol Stream, Ill.: Hope Publishing Company, 1982), no. 39.

8. C. Wesley, "See, Jesu, Thy Disciples See," *Collection of Hymns*, no. 474.

Chapter 7

1. J. Ernest Rattenbury, *The Eucharistic Hymns of John and Charles Wesley* (London: Epworth Press, 1948), 20–30.

2. C. Wesley, "God of Unexampled Grace," in Rattenbury, *The Eucharistic Hymns*, no. 21.203.

3. Ibid., no. 21.7, italics added.

4. Douglas V. Steere, *Gleanings: A Random Harvest* (Nashville, Tenn.: Upper Room Books, 1986), 83.

5. C. Wesley, "God of Unexampled Grace," no. 21.1–3, 7–9.

Chapter 8

1. Thomas à Kempis, *The Imitation of Christ*, ed. Harold C. Gardiner (Garden City, N.Y.: Image Books, 1955), 224–25.

2. C. Wesley, "Jesu, Suffering Deity," in Rattenbury, *The Eucharistic Hymns*, no. 12, 1–2.

3. C. Wesley, "Sinner, with Awe Draw Near," in Rattenbury, *The Eucharistic Hymns*, no. 39.1, 3.

4. C. Wesley, "How Glorious Is the Life Above," in Rattenbury, *The Eucharistic Hymns*, no. 101.1, 4.

5. Gregory Dix, *The Shape of the Liturgy* (New York: Seabury Press, 1982), 48–50.

6. Frances R. Havergal, "Take My Life, and Let It Be," in *The United Methodist Hymnal,* no. 399.

7. "A Covenant Prayer in the Wesleyan Tradition," in *The United Methodist Hymnal,* no. 607.

8. C. Wesley, "Ah, Tell Us No More," in Rattenbury, *The Eucharistic Hymns,* no. 92.4, 7–8.

9. Ibid., no. 92.

Epilogue

1. C. Wesley, "Jesu, Thou Sovereign Lord of All," in *Collection of Hymns,* no. 285.

About the Author

Paul W. Chilcote is Professor of the Practice of Evangelism at Duke University Divinity School. He has been involved in theological education on three continents, serving as a missionary with his wife, Janet, in Kenya and as a charter faculty member of Africa University in Zimbabwe. Dr. Chilcote previously served as Nippert Professor of Church History and Wesleyan Studies at the Methodist Theological School in Ohio and more recently helped to launch the new campus of Asbury Theological Seminary in Florida.

Dr. Chilcote is the author of eight books, including *Praying in the Wesleyan Spirit* (Upper Room Books), *The Wesleyan Tradition: A Paradigm for Renewal* (Abingdon Press), and *Recapturing the Wesleys' Vision* (InterVarsity Press). He serves as a unit editor in *The Works of John Wesley* project, is president of The Charles Wesley Society, and enjoys a special relationship with Mount Angel Abbey in Oregon as a Benedictine oblate. Dr. Chilcote is a frequent speaker and workshop leader in applied Wesleyan studies, particularly in the areas of spirituality, worship, discipleship, and evangelism.

Art Credits

The Transfiguration by Raphael, Vatican Museums & Galleries, Rome / Bridgeman Art Library, London / SuperStock

Icon of the Holy Trinity by Andrei Rublev, Tretyakov Gallery, Moscow / Anatoly Sapronenkov / SuperStock

The Angelus by Jean-François Millet. Musée d'Orsay, Paris / SuperStock.

Return of the Prodigal Son by Fouquet © 2004 Artists Rights Society (ARS), New York. Photo Banque D'Images, ADAGP / Art Resource, NY.

Walk to Emmaus and *Gethsemane* by Dr. He Qi (www.heqiarts.com). Used by permission.

Pentecost © Vie de Jesus Mafa, 24 Rue Maréchal Joffre F-78000 Versailles www.jesusmafa.com.

White Crucifixion by Marc Chagall © 2004 Artists Rights Society (ARS), New York / ADAGP, Paris. Photography © The Art Institute of Chicago.